22562

PN
1993.5   Klingender, Francis
.A1   Donald.
K5   Money behind the
1978   screen

DATE			

MONEY BEHIND THE SCREEN

This is a volume in the
Arno Press collection

ASPECTS OF FILM

Advisory Editor
Garth S. Jowett

See last pages of this volume
for a complete list of titles.

MONEY
BEHIND THE SCREEN

F. D. Klingender and Stuart Legg

ARNO PRESS
A New York Times Company
New York • 1978

Editorial Supervision: MARIA CASALE

———◆———

Reprint Edition 1978 by Arno Press Inc.

Reprinted by permission of Lawrence & Wishart Ltd.

ASPECTS OF FILM
ISBN for complete set: 0-405-11125-8
See last pages of this volume for titles.

Manufactured in the United States of America

———◆———

Library of Congress Cataloging in Publication Data

Klingender, Francis Donald.
    Money behind the screen.

    Reprint of the 1937 ed. published by Lawrence
and Wishart, London, which was prepared on behalf
of the Film Council.
    Bibliography: p.
    1. Moving-picture industry--Finance. I. Legg,
Stuart, joint author. II. Film Council, London.
III. Title.
PN1993.5.A1K5 1978   338.4'7'79143   77-11378
ISBN 0-405-11134-7

MONEY BEHIND THE SCREEN

MONEY
BEHIND THE SCREEN

A Report prepared on behalf of
the FILM COUNCIL

by
F. D. Klingender and Stuart Legg

With a preface by
John Grierson

1937
LAWRENCE AND WISHART
LONDON

INTRODUCTION.

This analysis of film finance may seem in parts to touch the realms of fantasy. Its rich figures and the spectacular flutters with fortune which lie behind them, are, however, as near as we can make it, the truth of the matter. The story itself was published in outline in the January number of *World Film News* and not the least ardent of its readers was the intelligence section of one of the bigger banks concerned. Within a week came the news that the lavish credits till now advanced to the film industry, were to be brought under review.

It may, therefore, be a useful moment to publish the full account from which the *World Film News'* story was taken. It is the work of the Film Council, a small research group, which a few enquiring members of the film industry set up some months ago to study the social aspects of the cinema. We felt a lack in the information trotted out, and often very ably, in the trade papers, fan magazines and film columns of the newspapers. We wanted to look behind the gossip, rumours, hunches and half-truths of Wardour Street and create for ourselves a more satisfactory body of information. We were conscious—and who in the film industry is not ?— that many of the facts which we daily encountered in our work were considered by the journalists too hot to touch and that aspects of the film industry of great social importance remained unstudied.

At odd corners of the field we have Mr. Rowson doing able research on cinema attendances, Mr. Bernstein looking into the tastes of his suburban audiences, and the Film Institute holding a conference on the reactions of children ; but, unlike other great industries, the film world lacks an Intelligence Department. Matters of concern to its own commercial success, like the reaction of audiences in different communities and the conditions governing the market in other countries, and matters of social value like the development of the cinema outside the theatres, are more a matter of rumour than of solid knowledge.

This industry in which millions of pounds are invested and on which millions of people have come to depend for their spiritual sustenance, still operates, like any village grocery store, on rule of thumb ; and not all the thumbs are ' thumbs of gold.' Without denying the virtue of those hunches which must, in showman as in artist, press beyond calculation, this is an unsatisfactory state of affairs, which should be mended if we are to make the most of a great national opportunity.

It is the more dangerous to muddle along in an industry in which the difference between showmanship and racketeering is often slight and may pass in the confusion unnoticed.

At the Film Council our concern is the concern of creative workers for the medium in which they must work. Though some of us would hardly pretend to be economists, this finance story is the most vital of stories to us. With, say, fifty thousand pounds to spend on a picture it is important to know that only twenty thousand pounds will be left, after the extravagances and the rake-offs, to go on to the screen. It is not unusual for producers and directors to be kicking their heels because the financiers are too busy manipulating their shares. The creative worker lives in such uncertainty from day to day and from picture to picture that, in final cynicism, he as often as not joins the throng and, with his financial masters, maintains the principle of getting his while the getting's good. This perhaps will explain the uncreative presence of so many creative men in the wilderness of films.

If, through the Film Commission proposed by the Moyne Committee, order can be brought to the finances of our work, mismanagement eliminated and this rush of promoters abated, it is the creative worker who will most have reason to bless a measure of government co-ordination. We shall have lost an Arabian night's entertainment and many of us, who have too much of the cinema in our blood to dislike even its insanities, may shed a sentimental tear for the old mad days. But we shall, no question, get on with the work we want to do. Under the conditions attested in this story that is impossible.

JOHN GRIERSON.

January, 1937.

THE FILM COUNCIL,
    OXFORD HOUSE, W.1.

ACKNOWLEDGMENT.

The information presented in this report is mainly derived from the files at the Company Registration Office, from the pages of the financial and film trade press (especially the *Financial News, Financial Times, Stock Exchange Gazette, Investors Chronicle, Kinema Weekly, To-day's Cinema* and *Daily Film Renter*), from such standard annuals as the *Kinematograph Yearbook, Stock Exchange Yearbook, Directory of Directors* and *Who's Who*, and from the report and evidence of the Moyne Committee. We gladly express our gratitude to the editors of the *Kinematograph Weekly* and *To-Day's Cinema* for their valuable advice and assistance. No one endeavouring to investigate the economics of the British film trade can fail to feel indebted to Mr. Simon Rowson for his pioneer work in this field.

We are indebted to Mr. O'Brien, General Secretary of the National Association of Theatrical Employees, for permitting us to consult a report prepared for his union by the Labour Research Department.

The finance for a long and laborious enquiry was provided by *World Film News*.

In view of the time limit allowed by
law for the public registration of
changes in a company's affairs, all facts
and figures in this Report should be
assumed to refer to the position at the
end of October, 1936, unless otherwise
stated.

CONTENTS.

MONEY BEHIND THE SCREEN

I.—STRUCTURE.

A.—AMERICAN PREDOMINANCE.

1. The passing of the Quota Act (Cinematograph Films Act, 1927), while virtually creating the British production industry as far as feature films are concerned, did not, however, put an end to the predominance of the major American producers in the English market. Table I indicates the proportion of English films registered during each quota year since 1928/9, together with the quota percentage (based on footage) provided in the Act, and the total number of features (*i.e.*, films measuring 3,000 feet and over) and shorts released each year. After an initial drop, following the spurt of home production during the first year, the proportion of English feature films increased steadily from about 16 per cent. to just under 30 per cent., thus considerably exceeding the statutory quota figure. The legal possibility of registering long films as quota for foreign shorts has, however, resulted in a marked lag in the production of British shorts behind the quota percentage.

TABLE I.

Quota percentage, and percentage and total number of British feature and short films actually registered 1929–1936.

BRITISH FILMS REGISTERED.

YEAR ENDING MARCH 31ST	QUOTA % (LENGTH).	PERCENTAGE OF ALL FILMS.		TOTAL NO. OF BRITISH FILMS.	
		Features.	Shorts.	Features.	Shorts.
1929	7.5	18.9	18.1	679	829
1930	10	15.9	16.9	602	1,065
1931	10	17.9	5.0	681	1,058
1932	12.5	24.7	4.5	618	977
1933	15	24.7	4.9	643	841
1934	17.5	28.0	6.8	679	707
1935	17.5	28.3	8.2	667	820
1936	20	29.5	12.8	718	663

2. If we confine ourselves to feature films (Table II) we find that even to-day American features account for more than two-thirds of all films registered in this country, foreign features other than American accounting for only about 5 per cent.

TABLE II.

Percentage distribution of films registered from December, 1934, until November, 1935, and from December, 1935, until October, 1936, respectively, showing country of origin and main renting groups.

				FEATURES.		SHORTS.	
				1935	1936	1935	1936
I. All Films Registered		...	...	100.0	100.0	100.0	100.0
A. Films {	American Films	...	...	67.0	66.9	81.4	77.2
	British Films ...	...	...	28.1	27.9	18.0	22.3
	Foreign Films (other) ...		...	4.9	5.2	0.6	0.5

TABLE II.—contd.

		FEATURES.		SHORTS.	
		1935	1936	1935	1936
B. Renters	Gaumont British Distributors, Ltd., and Wardour-Pathé ...	15.8	9.8	9.9	13.9
	Other British Renters	20.8	24.3	23.1	20.5
	United Artists and General Film Distributors, Ltd. ...	2.9*	11.4	2.9*	15.6
	American Renters	60.5†	54.5	64.1†	50.0
II.	British Films Registered ...	100.0	100.0	100.0	100.0
	Gaumont British Distributors, Ltd., and Wardour-Pathé ...	26.7	15.4	27.0	36.8
	Other British Renters	23.6	25.2	46.8	29.7
	United Artists and General Film Distributors, Ltd. ...	4.2*	16.6	—*	9.0
	American Renters	45.5†	42.8	26.2†	24.5
	No. All Films	709	653	783	697
	No. British Films	199	182	141	155

* United Artists only.   † Including Universal.

3. This does not, however, provide a complete picture of American domination. In the first place not all the American films imported are the product of the eight major companies (Paramount, Warner—First National, M.G.M., 20th Century—Fox, Radio, Columbia, Universal and United Artists). American films handled by these companies amount to one half of all films *registered* in this country ; under the quota regulations these companies must however in addition distribute a specified proportion of British films, and these " quota films " actually amount to one-half of all films *produced* in this country, so that one-half of the British production is in fact quota production controlled by the English renting subsidiaries of the major American companies.

4. The remaining American films (one-sixth of all films registered in this country), on the other hand play an important role in the business of the English renting companies, practically all of whom handle foreign films as well as English ones, and these American films in fact amount to one-half of all films distributed by these English firms.

5. Until recently this American predominance was exercised through direct control only of the *renting* side of the English film trade. Only two companies (Warner–First National, here always counted as one firm, and Fox) had established English production subsidiaries, while the remaining firms contracted with innumerable independent English producers for quota films. On the exhibition side most companies confined themselves to the control of a pre-release theatre in London, and only Paramount had a circuit (at present numbering 14 halls) in various key cities.

6. At the same time it was true to say that there were only two serious rivals to these controlling American companies in the

renting and production sphere (Gaumont-British Picture Corporation and Associated British Picture Corporation) and the strength of these concerns was derived from their vertical organisation based on the control of extensive cinema circuits.

7. Until recently therefore, the structure of the English film trade could be summaried as follows :

(a) *Renting :* The major American companies held absolute predominance and distributed well over 60 per cent. of all films marketed in this country (American and British) ; two major British renters handled about twenty to thirty British films and a similar number of foreign ones ; there was a varying number of other renters, only three or four of whom handled more than ten films each, the remainder only renting occasional films.

(b) *Production :* two major English organisations (each with more than one unit), affiliated to the two main English renting concerns ; two production subsidiaries of American renters ; and a large and fluctuating number of independent English producers renting through the two major and the independent English renters and/or producing quota films for the Americans.

(c) *Exhibition :* two main circuits affiliated to the two main English renters ; a large number of independent circuits of varying size and quality (see section 19 devoted to exhibition) one of which was controlled by an American renter ; a considerable majority of single halls.

B.—RECENT TENDENCIES.

8. Within the last 18 months this situation has, however, been modified in certain material respects owing to a number of changes which enable us to forecast imminent developments in the structure of the British film trade and in the mutual relations of the British–American interests. These changes are due, in the first place, to the reinforcement since about 1933/4 of the English production sphere through the immigration of prominent producers from the now dislocated continental production centres ; secondly, to changes in the organisation of at least two of the main American renters ; thirdly, to changes in the control of the two main British vertical combines ; and fourthly, to increasingly marked tendencies on the part of the major renters to acquire theatre interests.

9. The first and second factors are closely interrelated and it is convenient to begin with the latter. United Artists differ from the other American companies in that theirs is a co-operative distributing organisation for the quality pictures of a small number of independent producers. This structure made it an easy matter to extend the organisation also to English producers of quality films, which could not merely fulfil the Americans' quota obligations, but could also, if good enough, find a market in America and elsewhere.

The material basis for production on an expensive scale was thus provided for English producers equipped for this task. During 1936 United Artists' English affiliations have been increased from two to eleven, very largely utilising the services of the continental producers and directors who recently settled in this country. At present the English producers in the United Artists organisation actually exceed the American producers in number, although the control of the distributing machinery remains in American hands.

10. The second American company whose structure has changed is Universal. Early in 1936, the control of this company passed out of the hands of its founder, Carl Laemmle, into that of a consortium in which, together with A. H. Giannini and J. Cheever Cowdin (American finance and aeroplane magnate) English interests are strongly represented. The English members of the new Universal board, J. A. Rank, the miller, and L. W. Farrow, are at the same time members of the holding company controlling an important new English renting concern, with very strong financial support, General Film Distributors, which distributes the output of a number of English production units which are similar in type and which in some cases actually overlap with those affiliated to United Artists. Another result of this change in the control of Universal has been that the former English renting organisation of this concern has been merged with General Film Distributors, so that here again the English quality films distributed by the latter serve as quota for the American Universal output and benefit by the international distributing facilities of the new joint organisation.

11. These developments which are of far reaching significance in the emancipation of British production from its former quota bondage are already reflected in the film registration data of the last few months. They are illustrated in Table II, which analyses the films registered (a) during the 12 months from December, 1934 to November, 1935 and (b) during the eleven months from December, 1935, to October 27th, 1936. Confining ourselves to British films only, we find that quality production for the two Anglo-American renters supplying a world market has risen from 4.2 to 16.6 per cent., and although this increase is largely accounted for by a transfer from the two main British renters of the former period, it has nevertheless also led to a reduction in the numerical preponderance of " quota quickies." Moreover, the effect cannot justly be measured by the number of films alone, since the change in quality (and also, of course, cost of production) is of very much greater importance. While the power of the purely American renters (now reduced to six) is still overwhelming, if all films registered are taken into account, the new Anglo-American renters have nevertheless already acquired a position in the renting and production sphere at least as strong as that of the two former main

English renters. Moreover, the position of the former is still further consolidated by developments that have taken place or are at present taking place in the *exhibition* sphere. United Artists have acquired an interest, said to amount to 50 per cent., in one of the most important and rapidly expanding circuits of quality theatres in this country (Odeon) ; and General Film Distributors, Ltd., are now building up a new circuit of their own having already acquired control, according to press reports, of some two dozen cinemas in various parts of the country. There is, moreover, a link between United Artists and yet another major circuit, the County Cinemas, Ltd., controlled by C. J. Donada and owning over 50 cinemas (July, 1936). Two United Artists directors and Donada are on the board of the Entertainments and General Investment Corporation, Ltd., of which another United Artists director and County Cinemas, Ltd., respectively are prominent shareholders. Entertainments and General Investment Corporation is the largest shareholder in County Cinemas of which G. Archibald of the United Artists is also a director. Finally, J. G. and R. B. Wainwright, producers formerly for Universal and now for General Film Distributors Ltd., also control a cinema circuit (now reorganised as London and District Cinemas, Ltd. with sixteen halls.).

12. Another important feature of the new situation is, that both United Artists and General Film Distributors, Ltd., are linked by numerous cross-relationships. The San Francisco banker, A. H. Giannini, one of the Universal voting trustees, is at the same time president and chairman of United Artists, while in this country several executives of General Film Distributors, Ltd., are on the board of British and Dominion Films, Ltd., one of the United Artists producers. British and Dominion Films also have a part interest in the new Pinewood Studios, closely linked to General Film Distributors, Ltd., through J. A. Rank, and used by several General Film Distributors production units. H. Wilcox, still connected with British and Dominion Films, Ltd., has established a production unit of his own affiliated to General Film Distributors, Ltd., while M. Schach produces for United Artists in his unit known as Trafalgar Films and for General Films Distributors, Ltd. through Capitol Films. Through British and Dominion Films, both groups are also in touch with Paramount, since British and Dominion Films produce the bulk of the Paramount quota.

13. There is a possibility that this new group of English quality producers allied to American renters, will be increased by at least one further member, again closely related to the present two alliances. A. H. Giannini is also a prominent voting trustee of the American Columbia organisation. In August of 1936 it was announced that Paul Soskin Productions, a new unit with strong support and also associated with a new studio enterprise

had contracted for the production of eight feature films for Columbia at a total cost of £500,000. The first film produced by Soskin was released through United Artists.

14. Changes in the control and the mutual relations between the two main English renters which have occupied the centre of public attention in recent months are by no means clear in their final results at the present time. Since 1928, the American Fox organisation has had a major financial interest in, though not control of, the holding company controlling Gaumont-British, and the move initiated by Fox and its close ally, Loew's Inc. (controlling M.G.M.) to obtain virtual control of Gaumont British Picture Corporation, Ltd., would have resulted in a powerful reinforcement of the tendency for Anglo-American production-distribution alliances which we have discussed (although in this instance, the preponderance of American interests would probably have been greater than in the other groups indicated.) At present this arrangement appears to have been dropped and to have been replaced by a close alliance between Gaumont British Picture Corporation, Ltd., and its British rival, Associated British Picture Corporation. The latter has already acquired a substantial block of shares in the Gaumont British Picture Corporation holding company and claims to possess an option on the controlling block. Control is still, however, retained by the Ostrers, and 20th Century Fox similarly have retained their share holdings. The ultimate solution of this triangular tussle remains to be seen. While present appearances suggest a closer collaboration between the two English concerns at the expense of the American interests, the opposition of 20th Century-Fox to the transfer of control makes it not improbable that the ultimate result may still contain some surprises as far as Anglo-American relations are concerned. The recent acquisition of a block of shares in Loew's Inc. formerly owned by the late I. Thalberg, by an English financial group (about 30,000 shares, valued approximately at £420,000) is stated to be entirely unconnected with this situation.

15. It is very probable that the relationship of the great renting concerns to the exhibition sphere will undergo a further marked change largely as a result of the developments indicated in paragraphs 11 and 14. It is reported in the trade press (*Kinematograph Weekly*, 29.10.36) that representatives of an American renting firm are already attempting to negotiate with independent circuits for the acquisition of control. Moreover, it should be noted that Paramount who already control a small circuit of super-cinemas, have joint management arrangements for all theatrical matters, excluding film bookings, with one of the largest independent circuits, the Union group of some 250 cinemas. Although the latter retain their financial and also film booking independence under this arrangement it would be

curious if this tie-up were compatible with any degree of indifference in so far as Paramount film bookings are concerned.

16. The tendency for Anglo-American collaboration is not confined to the major American companies and their British associates. In the last half year more or less long term renting arrangements, involving in some cases also the American release of English films, have in addition been made between certain American independent firms and some of the more important other English renter-producers both of feature films and shorts. Recent cases reported in the trade press are : Associated British Film Distributors contract with Grand National Films Inc., involving payment over two years of $2,000,000 for 34 pictures per annum and a guaranteed distribution of A.T.P. films in the U.S.A. (Grand National Films controls 32 American film exchanges) ; British Lion Film Corporation contract with Republic Corporation of America Inc., involving deposit of $250,000 with Chemical Bank of New York and liability for another deposit of equal size (at the annual meeting of British Lion it was stated that while the money for this deposit was borrowed from two of the company's directors at 6½ per cent., no interest was being paid on this deposit by the Chemical Bank ; debentures of British Lion had risen from £20,000 to £125,000 with a liability for another £50,000) ; Ace Films, Ltd., contract for sole distribution in Britain for shorts produced by Educational Film Corporation of America, fifty-two 2-reel comedies and fifty single reel shorts.

17. The present structure of the British film renting and production trade is summarised in the accompanying Table A.

TABLE A—THE PRESENT STRUCTURE OF THE BRITISH FILM TRADE (AUTUMN, 1936).

Renter.	American Affiliation.	British Production Affiliation.	Exhibition Affiliation.
(A) AMERICAN RENTERS :			
Metro-Goldwyn Mayer.	Loew's Inc. (MGM)	Various quota producers.	London pre-release hall.
Radio Pictures.	R.K.O. Radio.	Various quota producers.	
Warner & First National.	Warner & F.N.	Own subsidiary with studio in Teddington.	—
Fox Film Co.	20th Cent. Fox.	Fox British, Wembley & New World Pict., Denham.	—
Paramount Film Serv.	Paramount Inc.	British & Dominion, Boreham Wood studios and quota producers.	14 super halls and tie-up with Union Circ. (250 halls).
Columbia.	Columbia Pict, Corp.	Paul Soskin Prod. & others.	—

TABLE A—THE PRESENT STRUCTURE OF THE BRITISH FILM
TRADE (AUTUMN, 1936)—*Continued.*

Renter.	American Affiliation.	British Production Affiliation.	Exhibition Affiliation.
(B) ANGLO-AMERICAN RENTERS :			
United Artists.	U.A. Corp.	London Film Prod., British & Dominion Films Ltd., Criterion Film, Brit. Cine Alliance, Bergner-Czinner Prod., Trafalgar F. Pr., V. Saville Pr., E. Pommer Pr., Garrett-Klement Pr., Atlantic Films, Pall Mall Pr., Denham, Worton Hall & Pinewood Studios.	Participation in Odeon (about 150 halls) & County Circ. (about 50 halls).
General Film Distr.	Universal.	Pinewood Studios British & Dominion Films Ltd., H. Wilcox Prod., Capitol Prod., City Films, Universal-Wainwright,Brit.National Films, Cecil Films, Grafton Films, etc.	New circuit in process of formation.
(C) MAJOR BRITISH RENTERS :			
Gaumont-Brit. Distr.	(20th C.-Fox).*	Gaumont-British Pict. Corp., Shepherds Bush, Gainsborough P. Corp. Islington.	Gaumont - Brit. Circuit over 300 halls.
Wardour F. & Pathe Pict.	Various occasional contracts.	B.I.P., Elstree and Welwyn and other indep. units.	A.B.C. Circuit, about 290 halls.
(D) OTHER BRITISH RENTERS :			
Ass. Brit. Film Distr.	Grand Nat. Films Inc.	Ass. Talking Pict., Ealing studio., and indep. prods.	None.
Twickenham F. Distr. (incl. P.D.C.).	Various.	Twickenham F. Stud., New Ideal P., Hammersmith, J.H. Prod., Boreham Wood.	None.
British Lion Film Corp.	Republic Corp. of America.	Beaconsfield Stud., also Hammer Prod.	None.
Equity Brit. Films.	Various.	Various quota prods.	None.
Butchers' F. Serv.	Various.	Various indep. prods. in ass. with Butchers.	None.
Ass. Produc. & Distrib. Co.	Various.	Sound City Studios, U.K. Films & indep. prods.	None.
Ace Films (shorts).	Educat. Film Corp. of America.	Ace Films.	None.
Reunion Films.	Mainly Continental films.	Various indep. prods.	None.

23 other Renters distributed from one to six films (Brit. and/or Foreign) in 1936.
Total No. of Renters' Licenses issued 1935/6 : 65 ; total No. of producers of long
films in 1935/6 : 76.

*NOTE.—Gaumont-British are the only English company having their own
distributing organisation in the U.S.A.

18. An entirely new departure in the renting-producing sphere was launched in November, 1936 in the " Independent Exhibitors' Distributing Co." This is an organisation of some 300 independent cinema proprietors who plan to conduct a renting and producing organisation of their own in order to improve their competitive position as compared with that of the circuits for the booking of British films. Each member undertakes to book a certain number of the films thus produced, which are financed on the basis of this assured market. The organisation is thus similar in conception to the original First National Distributors company of America and it will be interesting to trace the effects of this venture, if successful, on the future structure both of the renting and exhibition spheres of the British film trade.

C.—EXHIBITION.

19. Changes in the exhibition sphere are as rapid as those in the other branches of the industry at the present time. There is no official census of cinemas, the number of licenses issued annually by the Board of Trade (4,855 in 1935) including a number of duplications owing to changes in ownership and other causes. The Board of Trade, however, estimate that the number of cinemas showing regular programmes in the U.K. is 4,400 (summer 1936), as compared with about 3,000 in 1926. (Moyne Committee Evidence.) S. Rowson estimated the number at the end of 1934 at 4,305 and according to the Cinematograph Exhibitors' Association the net increase during 1935 was 92, which brings the figure approximately up to the Board of Trade estimate. Of this increase 27 were stated to be circuit halls, the remainder being independent units (though no definition of " circuit " was given). S. Rowson estimated the total seating capacity at the end of 1934 at 3,872,000 ; we shall assume that the new halls brought the seating capacity by the end of 1935 to be about 3,950,000.

20. The *Kinematograph Yearbook* for 1936 contains a list of 159 circuits of two or more halls each, but it is probable that this list is incomplete as far as the smallest groups are concerned. These circuits controlled 1,887 halls, or 43 per cent. of the total (the figures must be regarded as referring to the end of 1935) The following table shows the relative strength of these groups .

Size or Circuit.	No. of Circuits	Total No. of Cinemas
1– 10 halls	128	615
10– 19 „	22	288
20– 49 „	4	130
50– 99 „	1	53
100–199 „	2	242
More than 200 halls... ...	2	559

It will be seen that there is a great difference in strength and number between the small, the medium sized and the large circuits. The position of the latter with regard to the number of halls and the seating capacity controlled at the end of 1935 was as follows :

The 9 largest circuits controlled :—

984 halls with 1,290,000 seats, or 22 per cent. of the halls and 33 per cent. of the seats in this country.

The 4 largest circuits : 801 halls with 950,000 seats, or 18 per cent. of the halls and 24 per cent. of the seats in this country.

The 2 largest circuits : 559 halls with 653,000 seats, or 13 per cent. of the halls and 17 per cent. of the seats in this country.

In order of size these circuits were : Gaumont-British Picture Corp. and its subsidiaries ; Associated British Cinemas ;' Union Cinema Group ; Odeon Theatres ; H. D. Moorhouse Circuit ; A. B. King ; County Cinemas ; E. J. Hinge ; Shipman & King. According to the Cinematograph Exhibitors' Association (Moyne Committee Evidence) 9 circuits controlled 652 first run theatres, amounting to approximately 50 per cent. of all first run halls, which in turn control the booking situation.

21. The two largest circuits are affiliated to renter-producer concerns, while the two next in size have some more or less definite link with renting organisations. Of the smaller circuits at least one is controlled by executives engaged in production (Wainwright) and at least two by renters (Paramount and General Film Distributors). Apart from the link indicated in paragraph 11 for County Cinemas, there is no evidence of joint interests between producers or renters and any other cinema enterprise.

22. Changes during 1936 have brought about a rapid increase in the size of the larger and medium circuits, while a number of smaller ones have crossed the 20 mark. It appears from notices published in the trade press that the four largest circuits alone have increased their total cinema holdings from 801 to 1,055 halls (approx.). If the total number of cinemas in the country has increased at the same rate as last year, this would mean that the 4 largest circuits now control some 23 per cent. of all halls (instead of 18 per cent. at the end of 1935). The combined strength of Gaumont-British and Associated British Picture Corporation, Ltd., is stated to be 635 cinemas or 14 per cent. of the assumed total. It appears reasonable to assume that the tendency most marked to-day is a decisive and continuous strengthening of the position of the major circuits, as compared with that of the single halls and of the smallest groups. (On the parallel tendency for closer links between renters and exhibitors see paragraphs 11, 15 and 18.)

II.—FINANCE.

A.—THE MAIN GROUPS.

23. (a) *The Gaumont Group*. The main company of this group is the Gaumont British Picture Corporation Ltd., formed in March, 1927*. This company itself owns a number of cinemas and has control of the following theatre circuits :—

Albany Ward Theatres.
Associated Provincial Picture Houses.
Denman Picture Houses.
General Theatres Corporation.
H. & G. Cinemas.
Provincial Cinematograph Theatres.
United Picture Theatres.
Gaumont Super Cinemas.

The total interest of the group in the exhibition sphere is at present reported to include over 300 theatres and cafes.

In the production sphere the company owns studios at Shepherds Bush and controls Gainsborough Pictures, Ltd., with studios at Islington, while educational films are produced by Gaumont-British Instructional Films (a subsidiary of G.B. Equipments, Ltd.), and news reels by the Gaumont-British News.

The distributing organisation of the combine is Gaumont-British Distributors, Ltd., which also has an American branch company.

British Acoustic Films, Ltd., International Acoustic Films, Ltd., and G.B. Equipments, Ltd., are equipment subsidiaries of the group which has also a substantial interest in the Baird Television Co., and in the radio industry (Bush Radio). Among its other subsidiary or associated companies are C. & M. Productions, New Standard Film Co., and Standard Film Co.

24. *Control*. Gaumont-British Picture Corporation Ltd., is controlled by the Metropolis and Bradford Trust Co., Ltd., which owns 2,915,000 Ordinary 10s. shares out of a total of 5,000,000 issued (of these shares 2,100,000 are held on behalf of Twentieth Century-Fox Film Corp. and 815,000 on behalf of three Ostrer Brothers).

---

* The original Gaumont business in London was founded in 1898 by Lt.-Col. A. C. Bromhead in the form of an agency for Leon Gaumont of Paris. In 1914 the Gaumont Co. constructed and equipped the first large modern film studios in London. In 1922 the Gaumont Co. came entirely under British control, the majority proprietory interest being acquired by Lt.-Col. Bromhead and his British associates. At the same time the Ostrer Brothers, hitherto known as merchant bankers, became identified with the concern. When in 1927 the Gaumont British Picture Corporation Ltd. was formed to acquire the Gaumont Co. Ltd., the Ideal Film Renting Co. and the W. & F. Film Service Ltd. with a group of 22 theatres (later expanded by further acquisitions to about 300), Lt.-Col. Bromhead was appointed chairman of the new company, a position from which he resigned in 1929.

Metropolis and Bradford Trust was registered as a private company in 1929 (having been formed as a public company in February, 1928), with an authorised capital of £422,500 in 10,000 " A " £1 shares (voting) and 1,000,000 " B " 8s. 3d. non-voting shares. The whole capital was issued by January, 1936, and there were no mortgages or charges outstanding. Its four directors are :—

> S. R. Kent (President Twentieth Century Fox).
> J. M. Wallace (Vice-President Chase National Bank, London branch).
> Mark Ostrer (Chairman).
> Maurice Ostrer.

The shares are owned as follows :—

" A " shares (Voting).	5,100 by Isidore Ostrer.
	4,700 by Twentieth Century Fox.
	100 by W. J. Hutchinson (Manager, Twentieth Century Fox).
	50 by S. R. Kent (President, Twentieth Century Fox).
	50 by R. B. McDonald (solicitor, Twentieth Century Fox).
" B " shares (non-Voting).	750,000 by United American Investment Corporation (for Twentieth Century Fox).
	250,000 by John Maxwell on behalf of Associated British Picture Corporation Ltd. (acquired in October, 1936, from Isidore, Mark and Maurice Ostrer).

According to the *Financial Times* of 21st October, 1936, the price paid by Associated British Picture Corporation Ltd for these non-voting shares was £350,000 in cash and an allotment of 300,000 ordinary 5s. Associated British Picture Corporation Ltd shares, or a total of £618,125 at the market value of the latter.   The price for the 5,100 voting shares to be acquired later (though at the present time the right to transfer these latter shares is contested by 20th Century-Fox) is understood to be £800,000.   The share of the Ostrers, if the deal is completed, would therefore be £1,418,125, or £1 18s. 11d. per Gaumont-British share controlled by them, as compared with a market value (21st October, 1936), of the latter of 16s. 9d.

25. *The Gaumont-British Picture Corporation Ltd.* board consists of the following members :—

> Isidore Ostrer (President).
> Mark Ostrer (Chairman and Managing).
> Maurice Ostrer (Assistant Managing).
> S. R. Kent.
> Dixon Broadman.
> O. H. C. Balfour.
> J. Maxwell.
> Col. H. A. Micklem.
> C. H. Dade.
> I. P. Little

The three Ostrers hold numerous directorships in associated film concerns, while the Fox interest is represented by S. R. Kent, O. H. C. Balfour and D. Broadman. The latter two are chairman and managing director respectively of Balfour, Broadman & Co., who are the Fox bankers in this country. J. Maxwell's other directorships are mainly confined to the Associated British Picture Corporation Ltd. group. Col. Micklem is chairman of the Alliance Investment Co., Ltd., the Army & Navy Investment Trust Co., Ltd., the Banker's Investment Trust, Ltd., and Greenwood & Batley, Ltd. ; he is also a director of the Chinese Engineering & Mining Co., Ltd., the Great Southern of Spain Railway Co., Ltd., the Sterling Trust, Ltd., the Zafra & Huelva Railway Co., Ltd., and other companies. C. H. Dade, a council member of the British Electrical Federation, Ltd., and of the Federation of British Industries, is chairman of Clayton Dewandre Co., Ltd., and Transport Power & Finance, Ltd., and director of Transport Hotels, Ltd., Electrical & Industrial Investment Co., Ltd., Ever Ready Co. (Great Britain), Ltd., Ever Ready Trust Co., Ltd., and of eight electric supply or transport companies. I. P. Little is a director of Geo. Adlam & Sons, Ltd. Viscount Lee of Fareham (former Cabinet Minister and at present chairman of Trinidad Lake Asphalt, Ltd., of Mount Magnet Gold Mines, Ltd., and of Youanmi Gold Mines, Ltd.) is vice-president of Gaumont-British Picture Corporation, Ltd. but, according to the *Financial Times* of 14th October, 1936, not a member of its board.

26. The authorised capital of Gaumont-British Picture Corporation, Ltd. is £6,250,000, divided into :

£3,250,000 5$\frac{1}{2}$ per cent. Cumulative 1st Preference Shares of £1.

£2,500,000 Ordinary 10s. Shares.

£500,000 " A " Ordinary 5s. Shares.

In addition, there is an outstanding issue of £5,160,000 4$\frac{1}{2}$ per cent. First Mortgage Debenture Stock, while the overdraft of the Corporation with the National Provincial Bank was stated by Mr. Mark Ostrer at the last annual meeting (2nd November, 1936) to be £1,149,785 (an increase of £482,000 over the previous year and compared with only £133,171 in 1934 ; of the present sum £247,904 was stated by Mr. Ostrer to represent borrowing for film production). This overdraft is secured by an additional First Mortgage Debenture issue of £1,340,000 in favour of the bank.

27. Apart from the controlling group already discussed, there are a number of financial, insurance and nominee companies with substantial shareholdings in Gaumont-British Picture Corporation, Ltd. The most important, from the point of view of the size of their holdings, are :—

	PRE-FERENCE £1.	" A " 5/-	ORDINARY 10/- SHARES.
Alliance Investment Co.	42,276	—	—
Army and Navy Investment Trust	37,276	—	—
Bankers Investment Trust	73,554	—	—
Bishopsgate Nominees	246,947	18,520	48,300
British & German Trust (on whose board a representative of the Prudential Assurance Co. sits side by side with one of the German Dye trust I. G. Farbenindustrie)	20,000	—	—
C. O. Nominees	—	—	62,500
Control Nominees	43,345	231,906	26,764
Equity and Law Life Assurance Society ...	35,454	—	—
Foreign, American & General Investment Co. ...	21,500	—	—
Foreign & Colonial Investment Trust	21,500	—	—
Granville Investment Trust	24,878	1,680	—
Greenwood & Batley (engineers)	29,276	—	—
London Office Royal Bank of Scotland Nominees	35,272	1,160	15,900
Various nominee companies of the Midland Bank	81,870	9,282	72,923
National Provincial Bank Fixed Holdings ...	—	—	41,100
Pearl Assurance Co.	32,511	2,000	5,000
Prudential Assurance Co.	125,000	—	—
Refuge Assurance Co.	25,000	—	—
Sterling Trust	35,000	—	—
Whitehall Trust	20,000	—	—

It will be noted that at least five of the companies of which Col. Micklem is chairman or director, hold prominent blocks of preference shares in Gaumont-British.

Among the countless individual shareholders the following are of interest :—

	5½% CUM. PREF. SHARES £1.	" A " ORDINARY SHARES OF 5/-.	ORDINARY 10/- SHARES.
Rt. Hon. Baron Aberdare	—	3,000	—
Sir Edward R. Anson, Bt.	2,000	—	—
Sir James G. Berry, Bt. (joint a/c with G. L. Berry and D. G. Berry)	—	2,256	4,640
Rt. Hon. The Countess of Birkenhead ...	—	—	2,000
Sir Edward H. Bray, C.S.I. (former partner Ogilvy, Gillanders & Co. & Gillanders, Arbuthnot & Co.)	—	—	5,000
Reginald C. Bromhead	2,045	—	—
Rt. Hon. Lord Camrose (B a/c, joint a/c with Lady Camrose, Hon. John S. Berry & Hon. Wm. M. Berry)	—	1,320	3,300
Ditto G a/c	—	1,160	2,900
Rupert E. Carr (Director Peak, Frean & Co., Ltd. & Associated Biscuit Mfrs., Ltd.) ...	—	—	2,000
Mrs. Maud L. H. Cazalet, joint a/c with Victor A. Cazalet, M.P. (member Committee Hudson Bay Co.), Peter V. F. Cazalet and Another ...	—	3,000	—
Foster F. Charlton, c/o " Daily Telegraph " ...	—	7,502	6,254
Sir Walter H. Cockerline (shipowner)	25,022	3,194	5,485
Lt.-Col. Wm. C. Cooper	—	3,555	—
Rt. Hon. Baron Cornwallis (Royal Insurance Co., Ltd.)	4,253	—	—

	5½% CUM. PREF. SHARES	"A" ORDINARY SHARES OF	ORDINARY 10/- SHARES
Sir James P. J. M. Corry, Bart. (of Cunard S.S. Co., Ltd.)	—	800	2,000
John A. Dewar (Director Buchanan-Dewar, Ltd., Distillers Co., Ltd., John Dewar & Sons, Ltd.)	20,454	2,000	5,000
His Excellency Cornelis Willem Dresselhuys ...	—	2,400	—
Thos. Greenwood (of the engineering firm, Greenwood & Batley, Ltd., of which Col. Micklem is Chairman), joint a/c with Charles H. Greenwood and Mrs. Edith M. Gordon ...	2,000	—	—
Sir John L. Hanham, Bart.	—	4,000	—
George L. Q. Henriques (stockbroker)	—	4,000	—
Capt. Humphrey G. Lambert, R.H.A.	1,363	8,120	14,000
Oswald Lewis, M.P.	—	—	6,000
Sir Frederick J. Marquis, J.P., of Lewis's Ltd., Director Martins Bank, Ltd., Royal Insurance Co., Ltd., etc.	—	—	2,500
Charles Micklem (stockbroker)	—	10,000	—
Brig. Gen. Wm. F. Mildren, C.B., C.M.G., D.S.O. (Director Amalgamated Press (1922), Ltd.) ...	681	1,000	2,500
James H. Newcomb (Director S. Japhet & Co., Ltd., and 11 other companies)...	6,818	—	—
Lionel H. Peacock	2,363	—	—
Stephen S. Ralli, c/o Messrs. Ralli Bros., Ltd., E.C.2	2,727	—	—
Sir Strati Ralli, Bart., c/o Messrs. Ralli Bros., Ltd., E.C.2 (joint a/c with Leonidas P. Argenti and Matthew J. Calvocoressi) ...	5,454	—	—
Walter Ritchie (joint a/c with James F. McGill)	9,545	1,026	2,565
Capt. Sir John C. E. Shelley-Rolls, Bart. ...	—	—	4,600
Richard W. W. Spooner (Director Kelly's Directories, Ltd.), joint a/c with John H. Bell	—	18,124	45,311
James E. Tomkinson (joint a/c with Geoffrey A. Barnett (stockbrokers)	—	39,593	—
Llewellyn S. V. Venables	2,727	—	—
Alfred R. Wagg (Chairman, Helbert, Wagg & Co., Ltd., British & German Trust, Ltd., etc.), joint a/c with the Hon. Walter B. L. Barrington (Director, Helbert, Wagg & Co., Ltd., and 12 other companies)	—	18,000	—
John Walter, (Deputy-Chairman "Times Publishing Co.," etc.)	2,000	—	—
The Rt. Hon. William Douglas Baron Weir of Eastwood (Chairman of J. & J. Weir, Ltd., Cathcart Investment Trust, Ltd., Anglo-Scottish Beet Sugar Corp., West Midland Sugar Co., Ltd., Director of Imperial Chemical Industries, Lloyds Bank, Ltd., etc., Vice-President of British Electrical & Allied Mfrs. Assoc., council member of Federation of British Induestries)	3,000	400	1,000
Hon. Ronald G. Whiteley	—	1,600	4,000
Allan H. Wynn (Chairman Mercia Estates, Ltd., Director, Barbados Electric Supply Corp., Ltd., Central Wagon Co., Ltd. and 12 investment companies)	—	2,000	—

The above lists are taken from the return made up to 11th October, 1935.

Prominent among the debenture holders of several Gaumont-British subsidiaries is the Law Debenture Corporation. The controlling interest in Denman Street Trust Co., Ltd., (holding debenture and preference shares respectively in Gaumont-British Picture Corporation, Ltd. and Moss Empires) has recently been sold by the Ostrers to an investment trust controlled by the Stock Exchange firm, Cazenove Ackroyds and Greenwood. The new directors are : Hon. E. Brand Butter-Henderson, C. Micklem, R. C. G. Chetwode, D. Schrieber and F. M. G. Glyn (partner of Glyn, Mills & Co.). Finally Sir W. A. H. Bass, Bart., is a director of Associated Provincial Picture Houses, Ltd.

28. The complicated financial structure of the Gaumont group, consisting as it does of the parent concern and sixty-four subsidiary companies, has rendered the Gaumont-British Picture Corporation, Ltd. statements of account increasingly unintelligible. At the last—and very belated—annual meeting, the shareholders accordingly insisted on an adjournment until a consolidated statement for the group as a whole, which had long been promised, could be presented. This statement was published on December 9th, and a week later the adjourned meeting took place. Again a group of the shareholders present advocated the rejection of the accounts, demanding the appointment of a shareholders' committee of enquiry. Shareholders also opposed four motions put to them by the board, and claimed to have gained majorities on a show of hands. On all these five issues the Board was, however, able to obtain decisions in accordance with its views. The following statement of the consolidated assets and liabilities of the group is taken from the *Financial News* of December 10th, 1936. The figures relate to the position on March 31st, 1936.

LIABILITIES.	£	ASSETS.	£
Share Capital	6,250,000	Cash at banks	431,424
Debenture stock and interest		Trade Debtors	260,629
accrued (ex-cl. inter-company holdings)	5,073,180	Payments in advance ...	113,885
Loan on Mortgages, incl.		Investments at cost less	
interest	50,428	amounts written off ...	11,029
Debentures and secured		Realised and unrealised	
loans of subsidiaries, incl.		productions in progress	
interest	1,301,339	at or below cost and ex-	
Shares of subsidiary com-		penditure carried forward	
panies not held within		in respect of future pro-	
group	5,292,622	ductions (excl. reserve of	
Bank overdraft secured ...	1,577,431	£200,000 for contingen-	
Sundry Creditors, Tax, etc.	973,706	cies)	1,378,908
Dividends payable to out-		Stocks and shares in hand	
side shareholders after		at or under cost ...	104,788
date of account	75,052	Investments in or amounts	
Surplus (excl. £200,000 re-		due from associated com-	
serve)	1,130,599	panies at cost less amounts	
		written off	1,136,539
		Ditto for 2 subsidiary com-	
		panies	216,897

LIABILITIES.	£	ASSETS.	£
		Fixed assets, incl. freehold and leasehold property, plant, etc.	16,273,149
		Sinking Fund Policies at or below surrender value ...	158,768
		Amount by which the aggregate cost of shares in subsidiaries exceeds appropriate proportion of the aggregate book value of the net tangible assets of those companies at the dates of purchase after making adjustment in respect of valuation of freehold and leasehold properties	1,638,341
	£21,724,357		£21,724,357

The *Financial News* (10th December, 1936) commented that the liquid position of the group as revealed in this statement was decidedly tight. Since, as against liabilities to sundry creditors of £1,048,758 and bank overdrafts totalling £1,577,431, sound liquid assets amounted to £921,755. The problematical nature of the value (£1,578,908) attributed to films in process of production was generally pointed out, as was the fact that practically all the fixed assets of the concern represent investments in real estate, etc., within the group itself. At the adjourned meeting, the chairman gave the following figures for the actual earnings of the group during the year terminating March 31st, 1936 :

	£
Depreciation and Sinking Fund	372,763
Debenture Interest and proportion of profits applicable to outside holdings ...	526,411
Corporation's Preference Dividends ...	178,750
Surplus (i.e., the earnings of the ordinary shares)	218,982
TOTAL	£1,296,906

Profits realised by the Gaumont-British Picture Corporation itself during the last six years are given in the following table (taken from the *Stock Exchange Gazette* of October 31st, 1936) :—

YEAR TO MAR. 31.	PROFIT. £	NET PROFIT. £	PREFER- ENCE DIV. £	ORD. DIV. LESS TAX. £	%	To RESERVE. £	CARRIED FORWARD. £
1936	715,514	375,506	178,750	—	—	200,000	147,021
1935	720,483	404,140	178,750	210,000	7	—	150,265
1934	692,214	419,170	163,750	210,000	7	40,000	134,875
1933	462,612	310,977	93,750	175,000	7	—	129,455
1932	490,301	326,350	93,750	120,000	6	79,833	87,229
1931	502,060	364,489	93,750	150,000	6	64,093	84,462

29. (b) *Associated   British   Picture   Corporation,   Ltd.* was originally registered in March, 1926, as a private company under the name of M.E. Productions, Ltd. In January, 1927, the company was made public and its name was changed to British International Pictures, Ltd. In October, 1933, British International Pictures, Ltd., was combined as a production unit with Associated British Cinemas, Ltd. (a theatre chain) to form the present company. Associated British Picture Corporation Ltd. is at present mainly a holding company owning the entire capital of Associated British Cinemas Ltd. (at present controlling over 290 cinemas), British International Pictures (now a private company owning the Elstree studios and controlling B.I.P. (Export) Ltd.), British Instructional Films (owning a studio at Welwyn), and the distributing units Pathe Pictures and Wardour Films. The main figure behind the formation of the combine, was its present chairman, Mr. J. Maxwell. Formerly a solicitor in Scotland he entered the film trade as an exhibitor in 1912, and later became associated with the renting business through Wardour Films, Ltd. At present Mr. Maxwell is also chairman of Madame Tussauds, Ltd.

30. The Associated British Picture Corporation board is as follows :—

John Maxwell (chairman and managing).	W. D. Scrimgeour.
Sir Clement Kinloch-Cooke.	M. A. Dent.
J. D. Bright.	R. G. Simpson.

Other directorships held by board members include (apart from Associated British Picture Corporation, Ltd. subsidiaries) : J. D. Bright :   City & Northern Trust Ltd., and Criterion Restaurants, Ltd. ;   Sir C. Kinloch-Cooke :   Colonial Mutual Life Assurance Society, Ltd. (London Board) ; R. G. Simpson, of Layton-Bennett, Chiene & Tait, chartered accountants : Chairman, Caledonian Gas Corporation, Ltd., London Scottish Investment Trust, Ltd., Pentland Investment Trust Ltd., Scottish National Trust Co., Ltd., Second Scottish National Trust Co., Ltd., Third Scottish National Trust Co., Ltd., he is also a director of the United Molasses Co., Ltd., J. & G. Cox, Ltd., Hailes Estates & Quarry Co., Ltd., and of ten other (mainly Scottish) investment trust companies.

31. The authorised capital of the company is £4,000,000 of which £3,550,000 is issued : £2,000,000 in 6 per cent. cumulative preference shares of £1 and the remainder in 6,200,000 ordinary 5s. shares. There is £3,500,000 5 per cent. first mortgage debenture stock outstanding (trustees : the Law Debenture Corporation). The largest single block of ordinary shares (1,596,000) is held by Cinema Investments, Ltd., a private company controlled and owned by J. Maxwell and four of his associates. Practically all the other

important ordinary shareholders are hidden behind investment or nominee companies, the most prominent of which are : Burlington Films, Ltd. (also a Maxwell company), 500,000 ; various nominee companies of the Commercial Bank of Scotland, about 460,000 ; of the Clydesdale Bank about 360,000 ; of the National Provincial Bank about 190,000 ; of the Royal Bank of Scotland, 161,000 ; and the Cinema Construction Co., Ltd., 200,000. Since October 12th, 1936, the largest individual shareholders of the company are three of the Ostrer brothers, with a total of 300,000 ordinary shares. Among the holders of preference shares the most important are : London Office Royal Bank of Scotland Nominees, Ltd., 77,000 ; London Nominees Union Bank of Scotland, Ltd., 35,700 ; and the Prudential Assurance Co., Ltd., 34,000.

The list of private people owning smaller blocks of shares in Associated British Picture Corporation, Ltd., includes :—

	ORDINARY 5/- SHARES	PRE-FERENCE £1 SHARES
Frank E. Butcher	2,950	—
Captain Edmund E. P. Combe, M.C.	2,000	—
Conway J. Conway, K.C.	3,000	—
Sir Clement Kinloch-Cooke, Bart., K.B.E., J.P.	4,050	—
Lt.-Col. Cecil G. de Pree	3,000	—
Rt. Hon. Lady Digby	2,000	—
Prof. John Fraser, F.R.C.S.	4,000	—
W. J. Gell (Pathé Pictures)	5,050	—
Captain Gerald R. de C. B. Guinness	2,250	—
Rt. Hon. Lady Hemphill	2,100	—
John Hitchcock	2,050	—
Ralph L. Jolliffe (Chairman, Bertram & Co., Ltd., Director, Booth's Distilleries, Ltd.)	2,000	—
Sir David R. Llewellen, Bt., J.P.	2,000	—
James Luke (Guard Bridge Paper Co., Ltd., J. Lovell & Son, Ltd., Vale Paper Co., Ltd.)	10,000	—
Rt. Hon. Lord Merthyr (Chairman, Kilgetty Anthracite Collieries, Ltd., Universal Building Co., Ltd., Director, Bonvilles Court Colliery Co., Ltd., St. Austell & District Electric Lighting & Power Co., Ltd.)	2,000	—
Walter Ritchie	13,900	20,095
Col. the Hon. Denis P. Tollemache	2,000	—
Edward F. Bowring-Walsh	2,600	—
Sir Ernest S. Wills, Bart. (of Imperial Tobacco Co.) ...	4,000	—
Sir Harold E. Yarrow (Director, Clydesdale Bank, Ltd., and Steel Co. of Scotland, Ltd., Chairman, Yarrow & Co., Ltd.)	2,000	—
Guy N. E. Kennett Barrington	—	5,500
Capt. Harold K. Salvesen (shipowner, Christian Salvesen & Co.)	—	3,000
Leopold Sutro	—	3,000
Wm. A. Workman (Chairman, Gracechurch Buildings Co., Ltd., Belbridge Property Trust Ltd., Managing Director, Gresham Fire & Accident Insurance Society, Ltd., and Gresham Life Assurance Society, Ltd., General Manager, Legal & General Assurance Society, Ltd., and Director of Aviation & General Insurance Co., Ltd.)	—	4,000

The above list is taken from a list of shareholders as at 27th August, 1936.

32. The total assets of the company on 31st March, 1936 were £10,510,043, of which £7,945,227 represented land, buildings, etc., and £545,972 film production.

Since the capital was increased to £1,000,000 in 1931, the profits and dividends of the company have been as follows :—

YEAR ENDING MARCH 31ST.				NET PROFIT. £	ORDINARY EARNED %.	DIV. %.	RESERVE. £
1932	...	...	...	109,831	13.5	5	65,000
1933	...	...	...	108,528	11.7	5	69,758
1934	...	...	...	273,591	13.4	6	—
1935	...	...	...	370,753	25.4	10	287,806
1936	...	...	...	639,851	46.2	12½	350,000

33. (c) *United Artists and allied producers :* Like the other American renting concerns in this country the United Artists Corporation, Ltd. is a private company controlled by the U.S.A. parent organisation.   Practically its entire issued capital of £7,500 is held in the name of Murray Silverstone, its chairman and manager. Its English board members are Sir Connop Guthrie, K.B.E., chairman of Lincoln Wagons & Engines Co., Ltd., and North Central Wagon Co., Ltd., and a director of Raleigh Cycle Co., Ltd., Rickett, Cockerell & Co., Ltd., Sturmey-Archer Gears, Ltd. and of London Film Productions, Ltd. (during the war he was the representative in the United States of the British Ministry of Shipping and a member of the United States Government's Shipping Control Commission, 1918) ; F. M. Guedalla, a solicitor and chairman of Central South African Lands and Mines, Ltd. ; G. Archibald, J.P. (secretary and treasurer) ; E. T. Carr and A. W. Kelly.

The interest of United Artists in the exhibition field (Odeon and Entertainments and General Investment Corp.) have already been indicated. In the production sphere they are allied by distribution agreements to the production units listed in the following paragraphs. They do not, however, directly participate in the production finance of these enterprises.

34. The most prominent United Artists' connection in this country is represented by the Korda group of companies concerned with the financing of London Film Productions and Denham studios ; it includes :

London Film Productions, Ltd., reg. 1932, issued capital £428,799 in 333,549 £1 6% cum. preferred ordinary shares and 1,905,000 deferred ordinary 1/- shares. Total registered indebtedness of the company £1,794,222 (figures refer to 31st December, 1936).
L.F.P. Trust Ltd. reg. August, 1934, capital £10,000 in 1/- shares.
Denham Studios Ltd., reg. July, 1935, £10 capital in £1 shares.
Denham Films Ltd., reg. July, 1935, capital £10 in £1 shares.
Denham Film Corp. Ltd., reg. July, 1935, capital £10 in £1 shares.
London & Denham Film Co. Ltd., reg. July, 1935, capital £10 in £1 shares.
Denham Securities Ltd., capital £52,500 in 45,000 £1 6% pref. and 150,000 1/- ordinary shares. The board of this company includes two directors of C. T Bowring & Co. (Ins.) Ltd., and one Lloyds underwriter (C. S. Crawley).

John Maxwell, Chairman, Associated British
Picture Corp. Ltd., Director, Gaumont-British
Picture Corporation Ltd.

Colin F. Campbell
(Chairman, National
Provincial Bank)

Sir John Ellerman

Denham Laboratories Ltd., reg. Jan., 1936, with £100,000 capital which was increased to £170,000 in November, 1936. In Jan., 1936, 29,998 ord. shares were allotted to London Films and 40,000 pref. and 10,000 ord. shares to the New Trading Co., Ltd.
Harefield Investment Trust Ltd. (capital £1,000, reg. July, 1936).
United Kingdom Picture Co. Ltd. (capital £50,000, registered May, 1935).
The Korda group is also concerned in the English organisation known as Techni-colour Ltd., registered in July, 1935, with a capital of £660,000 in £1 shares.

The London Film Production board consists of :—

A. Korda	Chairman and Managing-Director of L.F.P. Trust, Ltd., etc.
Sir Connop Guthrie	Director, United Artists Corp. (see para. 33)
H. A. Holmes ...	Director, United Kingdom Picture Corp.
E. Stevinson ...	Director, C. T. BOWRING & Co. (INSURANCE) LTD.
J. R. Sutro ...	Director, L.F.P. Trust Ltd.
C. H. Brand	Director, Technicolour Ltd.

The share list of the company, dated 31st December, 1936, shows that its largest shareholder is the Prudential Assurance Co., Ltd., with 25,000 deferred ordinary and 250,000 preferred ordinary shares. Among the other shareholders are :—

	Pref. £1	Def. 1/-
L.F.P. Trust, Ltd. (of which Mr. A. Korda is the largest shareholder)	2,500	397,701
Lloyds Bank City Office Nominees, Ltd.	—	1,000,000
Midland Bank (Princes St.) Nominees, Ltd. ...	—	325,000
Clydesdale Bank (London) Nominees, Ltd. ...	—	90,000
C. T. Bowring & Co. (Ins.), Ltd.	5,333	—
Sir E. R. Bowring	1,333	—
L. Bowring Stoddart, Jnr.	400	—
E. Stevinson	3,733	10,000
F. W. Stevinson	400	—
Mary Stevinson	666	—
W. E. Hargreaves	1,333	—
J. F. Gault (Insurance Broker)	1,333	—
Sir C. Guthrie	—	10,000
H. A. Holmes	—	20,000
C. H. Brand	—	5,000
C. S. Crawley (Lloyds Underwriter)	—	5,000
Various members of the Sutro family	50,000	1
L. Toeplitz de Grand Ry.	—	1
A. Korda	1,054	301

Among the creditors of the company the Prudential Assurance Co., Ltd., also appears to occupy the first place. On October 12th, 1936, that concern took up a new debenture issue secured on the company's undertaking and certain real estate (amount not specified: " all money due, etc.", but an enclosed schedule refers to earlier advances of £500,000 and £82,200 respectively, the latter secured on 54,680 Technicolour shares). Another debenture issue of £274,701 16s. 1d. was taken up on October 14th, 1936, by C. T. Bowring & Co. (Insurance), Ltd.

The statement of accounts of London Film Productions, Ltd., for the period from April 28th, 1935, to May 2nd, 1936, was summarised as follows in the *Kinematograph Weekly* of December 17th, 1936 :—

" Accounts of London Film Productions show that during the period to May 2nd, 1936, the company operated at a loss of £330,842 which increased the debit balance to £368,973 against an issued share capital of £428,549. Expenses of £113,017 incurred while the company was awaiting the completion of studios have been carried to Development Account.

" In addition to the capital there is a First Debenture stock of £500,000, a loan of £453,562, secured on a further Debenture and other secured loans totalling £549,291, while creditors amount to £288,892.

" Total assets amount to £2,229,973, of which completed productions and costs applicable to future productions account for £751,845. Property and equipment are valued at £564,149.

" There are a number of intangible assets including £19,250 compensation paid for cancellation of a contract ; £12,500 commission in respect of shares issued ; £94,885 Debenture discount account. Debtors amount to £41,408 and cash to £5,403."*

Apart from the interests indicated in the directors' and shareholders' lists, the recent re-organisation of Denham Laboratories may perhaps afford some clues to the sources of Korda finance at the present time. For in addition to A. Korda, E. H. George and C. H. Brand, the directors of that company are S. G. Warburg (a partner of M. M. Warburg & Co., Hamburg and Warburg & Co., Amsterdam, the continental banking houses related through the Warburg family with the New York bankers, Kuhn, Loeb & Co.), and D. Oliver (director of Grundwert A.G., Hamburg). D. Oliver and A. Korda are also director and chairman respectively of the Harefield Investment Trust, Ltd.

35. The next United Artists producer, British and Dominion Film Corporation, Ltd., was registered in February, 1928, to acquire the business of British Dominions Films, Ltd. Its present issued capital consists of £500,000 in ordinary £1 shares. It is reported to have a 50 per cent. control and shareholding interest ** in the Pinewood Studios, Iver, sponsored by J. A. Rank and C. Boot (see General Film Distributors, Ltd., group, para. 38) and a ten-year management agreement for those studios. The following are directors of British and Dominion Films, Ltd. :—

E. R. Crammond (Chairman).
C. M. Woolf (Managing).
H. S. Wilcox.
Capt. the Hon. R. Norton.
W. H. Cockburn.

E. R. Crammond is joint managing director of British Shareholders Trust, Ltd. and a director of English National Investment

---

* Another item appearing among the assets of this statement of accounts is : " Policies on the life of Mr. A. Korda (premium paid) £7,354."

** But see analysis of Pinewood Studios, paragraph 40.

Trust, Ltd., and National Canning Co., Ltd. C. M. Woolf and H. Wilcox are prominently associated with the General Film Distributors—Universal group of companies. W. H. Cockburn is also a director of Thomas & Evans, Ltd.

None of the individual shareholders listed control as much as four per cent. of the capital, the largest holding being registered in the name of the Midland Bank (Threadneedle Street) Nominees Ltd. (18,190). A number of other bankers nominees companies and investment trusts hold between 2,000 and 4,000 shares each. Individual shareholders listed include :—

	ORDINARY SHARES.
Norris M. Agnew, Esq., and another (Director, Bradbury Agnew & Co. Ltd., proprietors of " Punch ")	3,000
Leopold Albu (South African mining magnate and Chairman of Phœnix Oil companies)	3,008
James L. Ambler	3,785
Richard M. Beech	5,850
Mrs. Kathleen Bowhill and others	3,150
Leonard A. Bremner	2,340
Noel B. Brooks, M.C., and another (Chairman, Bolsover Collieries Ltd.)	2,000
The Rt. Hon. Earl of Carnarvon	3,900
Robert R. Crewdson (Director, Horrockses, Crewdson & Co. Ltd., Power-Gas Corporation Ld., Chattanooga Co. Ld., Mazapil Copper Co., Ld.)	2,000
Reginald G. B. Evans	5,350
Russell E. Fawcus (Director, Hartley Cooper & Co., Ltd.)	3,800
Sir Edward Holt, Bt. (Governor Joseph Holt, Ltd., brewers)	2,000
Sir Follett Holt, K.B.E. (Chairman or Director of 19 companies, incl. Barclays Bank, South American banking, railway, meat, etc., companies, Pullman Car Co., Ltd.)	2,000
Robert G. MacMillan (of Lloyds)	2,000
Sir Frederick J. Marquis, J.P. (Director or Managing-Director of Lewis's Bank Ltd. (this bank itself also holds 6,790 shares), Lewis's Investment Trust Ltd., Lewis's Ltd. (the retail stores), Liverpool and London and Globe Insurance Co., Ltd., Martin's Bank Ltd., Royal Insurance Co., Ltd., and 6 other companies)	3,000
Francis Redfern (Director, Distillers Co., Ltd., and 5 bottle manufacturing companies)	2,450
Sir Frederick H. Richmond, Bt. (Chairman, Debenhams Ltd., Harvey, Nichols & Co., Ltd., Newquay Knitting Co., Ltd., and Director of Royal Exchange Assurance)	2,000
Miss Lavinia S. Smith	4,680
Miss Maud Soward	5,850
Sir Kenneth D. Stewart, K.B.E. (Director, Thorne & Co., Ltd., Manchester Ship Canal Co.)	2,000
Miss Dorothy M. Stonard	2,340
Lieut. Humphrey H. Sykes	2,500
Ernest Taylor (Managing-Director, British Can Co., Ltd.)	2,000
Lieut.-Col. Franklin Thomasson (Director, First Garden City Ltd., etc.)	2,000
Harold R. Turner (Chairman, Ferodo Ltd. ; Vice-Chairman, Turner & Newall Ltd. ; Director, Rhodesian & General Asbestos Corp. Ltd.)	3,000
Samuel Turner, J.P. (Chairman, Turner & Newall Ltd., Samuel Turner & Co., Turner Bros. Asbestos Co., Ltd., Raw Asbestos Distributors Ltd. ; Director, District Bank Ltd.)	2,000
Ernest Tweedale	4,000
Alfred Watkin (Director, Martins Bank Ltd., London & Lancashire Insurance Co., Ltd., Manchester Liners Ltd., Manchester Ship Canal Co. ; Chairman, Lloyds Packing Warehouses Ltd.) ...	2,000

(The above are taken from sharelist dated 1.1.1936.)

36. The third studio enterprise associated with the United Artists group is Worton Hall Studios Ltd., registered in January, 1936, as a £10,000 company (in £1 shares) with A. S. Cunningham Reid, M.P., Marcel Hellman, D. Fairbanks, Jr., and A. G. Smith as directors and F. M. Guedalla as solicitor. Paul Czinner resigned from his directorship on 26th August, 1936.

37. Like the majority of independent producers in this country the other United Artists producers are private companies with very small capital resources of their own, their productions being financed by short term loans. This method of financing is discussed in Section B (para. 47, p. 48). The units in question with their capital and directors are as follows :—

ATLANTIC FILM PRODUCTIONS LTD.—Reg. November, 1935, capital £30,000. Directors : D. E. Brown (Insurance Official), T. Dodds (Solicitor), A. Esway, J. E. Jewell (Writer), A. Tolnay (Journalist) ; in addition to the Directors the shareholders include the Marquis H. C. Pallavicini (5,000 shares), J. McGowan (500), Mary Jewell (3,000 in addition to her husband's 11,140), Joan du Gurney (New York, 500), Sarah E. Fisher (500). Charges outstanding : £58,750 (Aldgate Trustees).

BERGNER-CZINNER PRODUCTIONS.—No details found, but Bergner-Czinner are concerned in FORUM FILM PRODUCTIONS LTD., reg. December, 1934, capital £5,000. Solicitor : F. M. Guedalla, and in INTERALLIED FILM PRODUCTIONS LTD., reg. July, 1935, capital £2,000. Directors : J. M. SCHENCK (Twentieth Century Fox), Dixon Broadman (Balfour & Broadman), P. Czinner, F. J. Clark, C. B. COCHRAN, F. M. Guedalla. (Produced " As You Like It," released through Fox British.)

BRITISH CINE ALLIANCE LTD.—Reg. August, 1935, capital £25,000 (10,000 ord. £1 and 15,000 6% cum. pref. £1 shares). Directors : Major H. A. Procter, M.P., Barrister and Conservative M.P., Arnold Pressburger, L. A. Neel (Director of Buell Combustion Co., Ltd. and United Water Softeners Ltd.), Max Schach, Vice-Admiral E. A. Taylor, one-time Empire Crusade M.P. and now Conservative M.P.

CRITERION FILM PRODUCTIONS LTD.—Reg. June, 1935, capital £10,000. With the addition of H. A. Jawes the directors are the same as those of Worton Hall Studios (see para. 36). Charges outstanding : £212,000 (Aldgate Trustees and Capt. Cunningham-Reid).

ERICH POMMER PRODUCTIONS LTD.—No details found.

GARRETT-KLEMENT PICTURES LTD.—Reg. March, 1935, £10,000 capital. Directors : R. Garrett and Otto Klement.

PALL MALL PRODUCTIONS LTD.—Reg. March, 1936, capital £10,000 ord. £1. There are also two debenture issues of £50,000 and £35,000 respectively (issued at 20% and 15% discount respectively). Directors : LOTHAR MENDES (Director, Lothar Mendes Productions Ltd.), H. B. Ham (Director of Myron Selznick (London), Ltd.), A. H. Smith (Solicitor of Herb. Smith & Co., Director of American Association Inc.), T. Kilbey (Company Secretary), and LORD PONSONBY (Under-Secretary for Foreign Affairs, 1924). Shareholders : Lothar Mendes (5,000), National Bank (Branch Office) Nominees Ltd. (4,998).

TRAFALGAR FILM PRODUCTIONS LTD.—Reg. January, 1936, capital £25,000. Directors : L. A. Neel and Max Schach (see British Cine Alliance) and A. B. Baxter. Charges outstanding : £450,000 (Aldgate Trustees) and a mortgage of £60,000 (Equity & Law Life Assurance Society).

VICTOR SAVILLE PRODUCTIONS LTD.—Reg. April, 1936, capital £10,000. Directors : V. Saville, J. Somlo and J. G. Saunders. Charges . £320,000 (Denham Securities).

38. (d) *The General Film Distributors Ltd.—Universal group.* General Film Distributors, Ltd., founded by C. M. Woolf after his resignation from Gaumont-British in June, 1935, has since March, 1936, been controlled by General Cinema Finance Corporation, Ltd· At the same time the English renting organisation of Universal Pictures, Ltd., was merged with General Film Distributors, Ltd., the controlling group also acquiring a prominent interest in the American parent company. General Cinema Finance Corporation Ltd., has a nominal capital of £1,225,000 (1,175,000 preference shares of £1 and 1,000,000 deferred shares of 1s.). Its directors are :—

THE RT. HON. LORD PORTAL OF LAVERSTOKE, chairman of the great paper concerns :—

Director⟨

Wiggins, Teape & Co. (1919), Ltd.,
Wiggins, Teape & Alex. Pirie (Merchants), Ltd.
Busbridge & Co. (1919), Ltd.
Alex Pirie & Sons, Ltd.
Allied Paper Merchants (W. T. & Co.), Ltd.
Annandale & Sons, Ltd.
Charles Morgan & Co., Ltd.
Commercial Union Assurance Co., Ltd.
Compass Investment Trust, Ltd.
Greaseproof Paper Mills, Ltd.

Through his mother, a daughter of the Hon. St. Leger Glyn and granddaughter of the first Lord Wolverton, Lord Portal is also related to that famous banking family (for Glyn, Mills & Co. links with Gaumont-British, see analysis of that company : Denman Street Trust and Witan Investment Co.).

JOSEPH ARTHUR RANK, D.L., J.P., of the Rank milling concern, whose directorships are :—

B. I. Transport Co., Ltd.
Birkenhead Silo Co., Ltd.
Buchanan's Flour Mills, Ltd.
Ernest Joyce, Ltd.
Horace Marshall & Sons, Ltd.
John Herdman & Sons, Ltd.
Joseph Rank, Ltd.
K.O. Cereals, Ltd.
Methodist Publications, Ltd.
Newsagents & Stationers' Supply Co., Ltd.
Pinewood Studios, Ltd.
Ranks (Ireland), Ltd.
Ranks, Ltd.
Riverside Milling Co., Ltd.
Roberts & Wrate, Ltd.
Springfield Stores, Ltd.
Universal Corporation of America.
Yoma (England), Ltd.
Yoma, Ltd.

PAUL LINDENBURG, the international banker, managing director of :—

S. Japhet & Co., Ltd.

Chairman
- Compass Investment Trust, Ltd.
- Hugo Kaufmann & Co.'s Bank, N.V. (Amsterdam).
- Industrial Finance & Investment Corporation, Ltd.

Director
- Fabrique de Soie Artificielle de Tomaszow (Warsaw).
- N. V. Nederlandsche Crediet en Financiering Maat.
- Oesterreichische Credit-Anstalt fuer Handel & Gewerbe.
- Roumanian Banking Corporation (Bucarest).
- Trust & Loan Co. of Canada.

LESLIE WILLIAM FARROW, chartered accountant, of Sissons, Bersey, Gain, Vincent & Co., who is also :—

Chairman
- Associated Paper Mills, Ltd.
- British Sudac, Ltd.
- Ford Paper Mills, Ltd.
- Indeuram, Ltd.

Deputy Chairman
- Car & General Insurance Co., Ltd.
- Motor Union Insurance Co., Ltd.
- Wiggins, Teape & Co. (1919), Ltd.

Director
- Alex Pirie & Sons, Ltd.
- Allied Paper Merchants (W. T. & Co.), Ltd.
- Annandale & Sons, Ltd.
- Charles Morgan & Co., Ltd.
- English Association of American Bond & Shareholders, Ltd.
- Great Universal Stores, Ltd.
- Grecian Marbles (Marmor), Ltd.
- Greaseproof Paper Mills, Ltd.
- International Combustion, Ltd.
- J. J. Ford & Sons, Ltd.
- Portals, Ltd.
- Royal Exchange Association.
- S. Lesser & Sons (1918), Ltd.
- Universal Corporation of America.
- Verellen, Ltd.
- Wiggins, Teape and Alex. Pirie (Merchants), Ltd.
- Winton Trust, Ltd.

LORD LUKE OF PAVENHAM, chairman and managing director of :—

Bovril, Ltd.
Argentine Estates of Bovril, Ltd.

Chairman
- Bovril Australian Estates, Ltd.
- Estates Control, Ltd.
- Santa Fee Land Co., Ltd.
- Virol, Ltd.

Deputy-Chairman Ashanti Goldfields, Ltd.

Director
- Australian Mercantile, Land & Finance Co., Ltd.
- Bibiani (1927), Ltd.
- Forestal Land, Timber & Railways Co., Ltd.
- Lloyds Bank, Ltd.
- National Bank of Australasia, Ltd.
- Sir Isaac Pitman & Sons, Ltd.

The five General Cinema Finance Corporation directors thus together hold some 75 directorships in large-scale financial or industrial undertakings and it is very doubtful whether any other English film group would present a similar array of finance-capital magnates.

The following particulars of shareholders have been filed :—

	PREFERRED	DEFERRED
LIST APRIL 8TH, 1936.	£1.	1/-.
Heathfield Investment Society Ltd.	137,783	87,670
Industrial Finance & Investment Corporation, Ltd. ...	112,784	52,670
Portals, Ltd.	137,783	92,670
LIST 25TH MAY, 1936.		
Heathfield Investment Society, Ltd.	50,000	45,000
Industrial Finance & Investment Corporation Ltd. ...	75,000	85,000
Portals, Ltd.	55,000	45,000
C. M. Woolf	55,000	155,000
LIST SEPTEMBER 18TH, 1936.		
Midland Bank (Princes Street), Nominees, Ltd. ...	53,722	32,230

39. All the General Cinema Finance Corporation, Ltd., directors, except Lord Luke, reappear on the board of General Film Distributors, Ltd., but in addition there are C. M. Woolf (see British & Dominion Films, Ltd., para. 35) ; M. Woolf ; L. A. Neel (see British Cine Alliance & Trafalgar Prod., para. 37) ; S. F. Ditchman ; and, as alternative directors, R. F. Norland, secretary of the Industrial Finance & Investment Corporation, Ltd., and director of Davy Bros., Ltd. ; and B. C. Gain, of Sissons, Bersey, Gain, Vincent & Co., director of Boyden Smith, Ltd., Brown, Stewart & Co., Ltd., and P. Garnett & Son, Ltd. The capital of General Film Distributors, Ltd., is £270,000 divided into 250,000 participating preference shares of £1 and 400,000 deferred shares of 1s. 249,990 preference and 399,990 deferred shares are held by General Cinema Finance Corporation, the remaining 10 of either group by Industrial Finance and Investment Corporation (2nd October, 1936).

40. The most important studio enterprise associated with members of the group is Pinewood Studios, Ltd.,registered in August, 1935. (See also British & Dominion Films, para. 35), and owning a four-floor studio plant completed in 1936. The nominal capital of this company is £300,000, of which £175,000 was taken up by October, 1936. The capital is divided into 50,000 each " A," " B " and " D " and 150,000 " C " ordinary £1 shares. There is also a charge of £300,000 in favour of Equity & Law Life Insurance Society. All the directors of British & Dominion Film Corporation Ltd., are on the board of the company in addition to its founders, J. A. Rank and Charles Boot, J.P., a large scale engineering and building magnate.

C. Boot is chairman of :—

Henry Boot & Sons, Ltd. (Sheffield).
    ,,   ,,   ,, (Overseas) Ltd.
    ,,   ,,   ,, (Garden Estates), Ltd.

Barnsley Syndicate, Ltd.
First National Housing Trust, Ltd.
Inter Counties, Ltd.

Director
- Anglo-Foreign Construction Syndicate, Ltd.
- Bedford Brick Co., Ltd.
- Bletchley Flettons, Ltd.
- Burnt Oak Estates, Ltd.
- Digswell Nurseries, Ltd.
- Flettons, Ltd.
- Cambell Rouse & Snoaden, Ltd.
- Hall & Son (Automobiles), Ltd
- Handside Houses, Ltd.
- Herts Gravel & Brickworks, Ltd.
- Howardsgate Investment Trust, Ltd.
- Playhouses, Ltd.
- Welwyn Buildings, Ltd.
-      "   Commercial Buildings, Ltd.
-      "   Garden City Electricity Supply Co., Ltd.
-      "   "   "   Ltd.
-      "   Stores (1929), Ltd.
-      "   Transport, Ltd.

Nor does this list completely enumerate the Pinewood board. There are three other directors : John Corfield, a director of British National Films, Ltd. (see para. 41), Harold G. Judd, chartered accountant, of Mann, Judd, Gordon & Co., who combines his Pinewood directorate with 8 chairmanships and 12 other directorships :—

Chairman
- Colortone Holdings, Ltd.
- Dunderland Iron Ore Co., Ltd.
- Equipment Trust Co., Ltd.
- Merchandising & Service Corporation, Ltd.
- Scottish Insurance Corporation, Ltd. (London board).
- Western Dominion Collieries, Ltd.
- Whessoe Foundry & Engineering Co., Ltd.

Director
- Bankers Commercial Security Co., Ltd.
- Christian Police Trust Corporation, Ltd.
- Dufay-Chromex, Ltd.
- Dufaycolor, Ltd.
- Entores, Ltd.
- First City Trust, Ltd.
- Girls' Education Co., Ltd.
- H. J. Enthoven & Sons, Ltd. (Lead merchants).
- Isteg Steel Products, Ltd.
- Mercantile Credit Co., Ltd.
-      "   Union Guarantee Co., Ltd.
- Robinson Bindley Processes, Ltd.
- Tati Co., Ltd.

The last member of the list, Spencer Mortimer Reis, appears to be a director of only the Pinewood Studios, Ltd.

The Pinewood share list shows the following principal shareholders :—

Henry Boot (Garden Estates), Ltd. (" A " shares, 49,999).
British & Dominion Film Corporation, Ltd. (" C " shares, 75,000).
British National Films, Ltd. (" B " shares, 49,998).

MONEY BEHIND THE SCREEN

41. In 1936 (first 10 months) General Film Distributors, Ltd., distributed films of the following producers (in addition to the American Universal output) :—

BRITISH NATIONAL FILMS, LTD.—Reg. July, 1934, nominal capital, £100,000, divided into 2,000 A, 2,000 B and 96,000 C shares of £1 each. Directors : J. G. Corfield (see Pinewood Studios), J. A. Rank, and Lady A. H. Yule (widow of the financier Sir Andrew Yule who left an estate of about £15,000,000). J. G. Corfield holds 250 C shares, J. A. Rank 1,999 A shares and Lady Yule 2,000 B shares. Mr. Rank recently resigned his directorship.

BRITISH PICTORIAL PRODUCTIONS, LTD.—Reg. February, 1926, capital £5,000, of £1 each. Directors : W. C. and C. W. Jeapes and A. P. Smith, who are also the only shareholders.

CAPITOL FILM CORPORATION, LTD.—Reg. September, 1935 (a Capito Film Productions, Ltd. was in existence since July, 1934), capital £125,000, in 5/- ord. shares. Directors : N. A. Procter, L. A. Neel, Max Schach (see British Cine Alliance and Trafalgar Film Productions, para. 37. Capitol Film Corporation has outstanding charges totalling £1,520,000 with Aldgate Trustees, Ltd., and £160,000 with Equity & Law Life Assurance Society (which latter concern has been allotted 8,000 of the issued ordinary shares, 200,000 being registered in the name of C.F.P., Ltd.).

CECIL FILM PRODUCTIONS, LTD.—Reg. December, 1921, as Fellner Films, Ltd., name changed March, 1924. Nominal capital £1,000 in 5/- shares, number of shares paid up, 16 ; of these, 8 by Capitol Film Productions, Ltd. and 4 each by E. Wolheim and T. Rowson. Directors : H. A. Procter, L. A. Neel, Max Schach, Herman Fellner and B. O. Schonegevel. Total charges outstanding : £415,000 (Aldgate Trustees).

CITY FILM CORPORATION, LTD.—Reg. July, 1934, capital, nominal, £1,000 in 5/- shares, of which 402 were paid up. Directors : W. G. D. Hutchinson, M.P., Lt.-Com. T. E. K. Donaldson (R.N., ret.), Capt. B. H. Humphrys, E. King. After guaranteeing 14 successive advances amounting in all to £233,150, the Aldgate Trustees appointed a receiver and manager for the company in April, 1936.

GRAFTON FILMS, LTD.—Reg. as British International Photophone, Ltd., in April, 1929, with J. Maxwell and some of his associates as Directors. They resigned in December, 1933, and in 1934 the company assumed its present name. The present directors are : J. H. MacDonald (Accountant), Capt. D. N. Gow (Director, Optima Films, Ltd.), J. Goldschmid (Film Producer), and G. W. Alexander (Accountant). The capital of the company is £100, of which £20 is paid up and there is an outstanding charge of £10,000 in favour of the Clydesdale Bank, Ltd.

HERBERT WILCOX PRODUCTIONS, LTD.—Reg. August, 1935 (an earlier company with the same name, reg. in 1925, was dissolved in 1934), capital £100 Directors : C. M. Woolf, H. Wilcox, M. Woolf, H. Hyman and J. A. Stephen.

J. G. & R. B. WAINWRIGHT, LTD.—Directors : J. G. & R. B. Wainwright. No further details found.

42. (e) *The Associated British Film Distributors group*. Associated British Film Distributors, Ltd., is owned and controlled by the producing company, Associated Talking Pictures, Ltd., a company formed in May, 1929, with an authorised capital of £125,000, £81,546 of which is issued in 5s. shares. There is also a 5 per cent.

redeemable participating debenture issue of £24,000 and another
debenture issue of £134,000 outstanding. The directors are :—

Basil Dean (Chairman).
Major J. S. Courtauld, M.C., M.P., (Joint Managing).
S. L. Courtauld (Joint Managing).
R. F. Ould (Joint Managing).
R. P. Baker (Chartered Accountant).

Basil Dean is also a director of Dean & Reed, Ltd., and Raycol
British Corporation. J. S. Courtauld (brother of Samuel Courtauld,
chairman of Courtaulds, Ltd.), and S. L. Courtauld are directors of
Raycol British Corporation, and the latter also of Slough Estates
and three tin companies. R. F. Ould, a barrister, is a director of
Parsons, Fletcher & Co. Basil Dean, with 52,700 shares, is the
largest shareholder in A.T.P. and there is a bank overdraft of
£163,403 with the National Provincial Bank. The company controls
the A.T.P. Studios at Ealing.

43.   During the first ten months of 1936, the following production units (other than A.T.P.) have released films through Associated
British Film Distributors, Ltd. :—

ALEXANDER FILM PRODUCTIONS, LTD.—Director : R. H. Alexander,
using Rock Studio. Capital, £100 in 10/- shares.

FRANCO-LONDON FILMS, LTD.—Directors : F. Deutschmeister, R. S.
Streeman, M. T. Harroway ; capital, £5,000 in 1/- shares, 99,978 of which
are controlled by the Société de Crédit pour l'Industrie et le Commerce, Paris ;
there are also insured overdrafts with the Chase National Bank and Martins
Bank. Studios used, A.T.P.

JOE ROCK PRODUCTIONS, LTD. AND LESLIE FULLER PRODUCTIONS,
LTD.—Directors : Joe Rock (U.S. Citizen, Managing), J. H. & H. F. B. Iles,
H. L. Goldby (the last three are also directors of Margate Estates, Ltd. and
other amusement companies) Capital : Joe Rock Productions, £100 in 1/-
shares owned by J. H. Iles and J. Rock ; Leslie Fuller Productions, £1,000
in 1/- shares owned by J. H. Iles and J. Rock. This group also own the Rock
Studios at Elstree, a £500,000 extension of which with 5 new sound stages,
was taken in hand in May, 1936.

PHŒNIX FILMS, LTD.—Owned by I.F.P., Ltd., reg. July, 1935. Directors f
J. Gray, H. Perceval, R. Denham and B. Mason. Capital, £1,000 in £1 shares:
500 of which are owned by J. Gray, the others being distributed equally be,
tween the remaining Directors. Charges outstanding : £103,000 in favour o-
Aldgate Trustees. Studios used, A.T.P.

STANLEY LUPINO PRODUCTIONS, LTD.—Owning Gaiety Films Ltd.
Capital £1,000. Directors : S. Lupino, J. W. O. Hamilton, V. F. A. Taylor.

TOEPLITZ PRODUCTIONS, LTD.—Directors : L. Toeplitz de Grand Ry
(Managing Director) ; G. Toeplitz (former Managing Director of Banca
Commerciale Italiana) ; Major W. d'E Williams, stockbroker ; Sir Charles
Petrie, Bart. (foreign editor *English Review*, member of War Cabinet, 1918–9,
advisory council member of the British Film Institute) ; and W. R. Creighton.
Capital (Nominal) : £100,000. Principal shareholders : S. A. Cunaris,
Switzerland, 84,000 ordinary ; L. Tœplitz, 10,000 ord. Charges outstanding :
£32,000 (Aldgate Trustees). Studio used : A.T.P.

Associated British Film Distributors, Ltd. also distributed
shorts made by the G.P.O. Film Unit and the Strand Film Co., Ltd.

44. (*f*) *The American Renters* not so far mentioned are without exception private companies controlled by their U.S.A. parent organisations. The British interests of Twentieth Century-Fox in Gaumont British and the cinema interests of Paramount have already been discussed. It is of interest that the Fox news reel service in this country, British Movietonews Ltd., is jointly controlled by Twentieth Century—Fox and the Hon. Esmond Harmsworth (chairman Associated Newspapers, Ltd., Daily Mail and General Trust, Ltd., and director of Imperial Airways, Ltd., and other companies). Of the 50,000 shares at 7/6, Fox hold 25,498, Harmsworth 21,500 ; the directors are : S. R. Kent and R. B. McDonald (Fox), Hon. E. Harmsworth and G. W. Price (Associated Newspapers) and F. L. Harley. Fox, Warner-First National and the Paramount News Service have studio organisations of their own in this country, while M.G.M. is now reported to contemplate British production in its own name, a £20,000 company having been formed for this purpose in November, 1936 (production to take place in the Amalgamated Studios at Elstree). Columbia has contracted for British films with Soskin Productions associated with the same studio enterprise and it is also noteworthy that the British organisations of M.G.M. and Columbia have one of their directors in common. Other interests represented by directorships of American renters' board members are : Moore's Modern Methods, Ltd.(C. F. Karuth of Paramount) : Equity & Law Life Assurance Soc., Ltd., Equity and Law Investment Trust, Ltd., Law Reversionary Interest Soc., Ltd., and Southern Publishing Co., Ltd. (R. F. Holmes, of Radio) ; and Electrical & Musical Industries, Ltd., Columbia Graphophone Co., Ltd., British Zonophone Co., Ltd., Marconi E.M.I. Television Co., Ltd., Marconiphone, Ltd., and Gramophone Co., Ltd. (A. Clark of Radio).

45. (*g*) *Other renter or producer groups* of interest are :—

BRITISH LION FILM CORP., LTD.—Reg. 1927, nominal capital, £210,000 issued 160,000 pref. ord. shares of 12/6 and 983,010 deferred ord. shares of 4d. Directors :—

> S. W. Smith (Chairman).
> Sir Rob. J. Lynn, M.P. (also a Director of Northern Whig Ltd., the Belfast newspaper company) ;
> I. C. Flower (also Director of Boosey & Hawkes, Ltd., Burt & Stevens, Ltd., Gloucester Hotel (Weymouth), Ltd., TWICKENHAM FILM FILM DISTRIBUTORS, LTD. ;
> N. L. Nathanson (Director of Regal Films, Ltd.) ; and
> A. P. Holt (Director of Brazilian Traction Light & Power Co., Ltd., British Columbia Power Corp', Ltd., Canadian & Foreign Investment Trust Co., Ltd., Dominion Tar & Chemical Co., Ltd., Famous Players Canadian Corp., Hydro-Electric Bond & Share Corp., Investment Corp. of Canada, Ltd. (Chairman), LONDON EXPRESS NEWSPAPER, LTD., Mexican Light & Power Co., Ltd., Montreal Trust Co., Scottish Grain Distillery Co., Ltd., Seager Evans & Co., Ltd.

All the main shareholdings are registered in the names of bankers nominee companies (Barclays, Lloyds, Midland and Royal Bank of Scotland), but the largest individual holding does not exceed 6,600 preferred ordinary shares. The company owns a studio at Beaconsfield and entered a joint production arrangement with Hammer Productions, Ltd., in February, 1936. (Hammer Productions, Ltd., incorporated 1934, is now a £5,000 company, mortgages outstanding £51,000, director and shareholders : W. Hammer, O. J. & G. A. Gillings and H. F. Passmore).

TWICKENHAM FILM STUDIOS, LTD.—Reg. 1929, capital (nom.) £33,500, issued : 21,500 preference shares of £1 and 240,000 deferred shares of 1/-. Directors :—

> Julius Hagen (Director, Real Art Productions) ;
> J. A. Carter ;
> F. P. and R. P. Philip (formerly Isaacs) (Directors of Twickenham Film Distributors).

The main shareholders are Leslie Hiscott (8,455 pref. and 187,794 deferred) and Margot Isaacs (4,600 pref. and 10,200 def.). There are also £35,000 mortgage debentures outstanding in the name of the Westminster Bank, Ltd. The company owns studios at Twickenham and Hammersmith (the former New Ideal Pictures studios acquired by Hagan together with P.D.C., Ltd.), and also controls J.H. Productions, Ltd., with studios at Elstree. Distribution is effected through TWICKENHAM FILM DISTRIBUTORS, LTD., a new company formed in May, 1935, with £55,000 capital in 50,000 6% cum. pref. shares of £1 each and 100,000 ord. 1/- shares. The following debentures or charges are registered in the name of C. T. BOWRING & CO. (INSURANCE) LTD., May 1935, £140,000 ; November, 1935, £110,000 ; October 1936 (supplementary) £150,000 ; December 1936, £34,500. A charge of £35,000 is registered in the name of H. G. Judd.*

SOUND CITY FILMS, LTD.—Reg. 1933, converted into public company 1935. Capital : authorised £350,000, issued £156,263, in ordinary 5/- shares and £135,000 in 6% participating preference shares of £1. There is also a debenture issue to Equity & Law Life Assurance Society, Ltd., covering advances up to £100,000 at 6%. Directors :—

> N. G. W. Loudon (Chairman) ;
> J. P. Steacy (also Director of Tiffany Valley Rubber Estates, Ltd., and Town & Country Estates, Ltd) ;
> L. G. Hill (also Director of Gilbert Films, Ltd., and U.K. Films, Ltd.);

Main shareholders :—

> Consolidated Nominees : 31,335 ord., 39,811 pref. ;
> Littleton Pink (Holdings), 277,910 ord. ;
> N. G. Loudon, 63,282 ord. ;
> S. Greenlees, 40,000 ord. ;
> F. R. Walker, 10,000 ord.

The company owns the Sound City studios, mainly let out to other producers. It also produces films through its subsidiary U.K. Films, Ltd., and has acquired all shares of Gilbert Films, Ltd., proprietors of Associated Producing & Distributing Co., Ltd., for £50,000 cash.

BUTCHERS FILM SERVICE, LTD.—Distributing American and English films mainly in the provinces (the latter usually made by them in partnership with various independent producers) is wholly controlled and owned by

---

*In December 1936, E. Stevinson of C. T. Bowring & Co. (Insurance) Ltd., joined the board of Twickenham Film Distributors, for whom a receiver was appointed by the former company on 9th January, 1937.

BRITISH PHOTOGRAPHIC INDUSTRIES, LTD. The latter company was registered in February, 1915, and owns, apart from Butchers F.S., also Austin Edwards, Ltd., Ensign, Ltd., Elliott & Sons, Ltd., Fordham & Co., Ltd., Houghton-Butcher Manuf. Co., Ltd., Houghton-Butcher (Eastern), Ltd., and Photo Supplies, Ltd. The Directors are : F. E. Butcher (Director of most of the above companies and of Fabric-meter Co., Ltd.), F. J. Butcher (Director of some of the above companies and of Butcher, Curnow & Co., Ltd.), F. G. Greenwood (Chairman of most of the above companies and Capener, Ltd. and Premier Film Printing Co., Ltd.), C. E. Houghton (Director of most of the above companies), E. W. Houghton (Director of most of the above companies), E. S. Houghton (Director, Elliott & Sons, Ensign, and Novelty Sales Services), I. Joseph, O. A. Dicot. Nominal capital : £1,000,000 ; taken up : 375,000 pref. £1 shares ; 600,000 ord. 6/8 shares. Principal shareholders :

	ORD. 6/8	PREF. £1
MAJOR THE HON. J. J. ASTOR (Chairman, Times Holding Co., Ltd. and Times Publishing Co., Ltd. ; Director, Hambros Bank, Ltd. ; Phoenix Assurance Co., Ltd. ; G.W. Railway Co., Ltd.)	13,000	20,000
VISCOUNTESS ASTOR	11,000	15,000
VISCOUNT ASTOR	7,000	5,000
F. E. Butcher	28,279	8,380
F. J. Butcher Bromley and 2 others	29,372	8,272
A. Edwards	27,123	12,550
E. W. Horton	13,726	8,845
G. A. Spratt	9,697	4,600
Mrs. Spratt and another	9,695	4,601
Higginsons Nominees, Ltd.	25,232	8,056

(Share list dated 9th July, 1936).

The last balance sheet presented in December, 1935, showed a net profit of £54 6s. 1d., there was no dividend on the ordinary shares (nor had there been any in the preceding year) and the dividends on the preference shares were stated to be in arrears since July, 1931.

AMALGAMATED STUDIOS, LTD. AND SOSKIN PRODUCTIONS, LTD.—New studio and production enterprises associated with the financier S. H. Soskin and the producer, Paul Soskin.

AMALGAMATED STUDIOS LTD.—Reg. as Miksos Trust Ltd. in October, 1935, name changed in November, 1935. Present Directors : S. Soskin, M. G. Soskin (both of Paris) and E. R. Gillingham (Solicitor's Clerk). Capital (nominal) £50,000 ; paid up : £9,245 in £1 pref. and £30,000 in £10 ord. shares, all of which are owned by S. Soskin. Charges : £180,000 secured on real estate in Elstree and Paris in favour of Sir Robert McAlpine & Sons (London) Ltd.

SOSKIN PRODUCTIONS LTD.—Reg. August, 1935, capital £10,500 in 10,000 6% cum. pref. shares of £1 and 10,000 ordinary shares of 1/-. Directors : S. H. Soskin (Chairman), Paul Soskin (Managing Director), Major C. H. Bell. Eight stages and administrative buildings are in process of completion and the production unit has obtained a £500,000 production contract covering eight films from Columbia.

46. (h) *The main Cinema groups :*

UNION CINEMAS.—The Union Group (Union Cinema Co., Ltd., Oxford and Berkshire Cinemas, Ltd., and National Provincial Cinemas, Ltd.) has in November, 1936, been consolidated into a new company, known as Union Cinemas, Ltd., with a total capital of £6,500,000, divided as follows :

	AUTHORISED	ISSUED
Redeemable 6% cum. 1st pref. £1 shares	2,000,000	657,406
Redeemable 6% cum. 2nd pref. £1 shares ...	1,500,000	657,406
" A " ordinary shares of 5/-	10,000,000	5,839,227
Ordinary shares of 5/-	2,000,000	1,960,421

The ordinary shares alone carry voting rights. Shortly before the details of the scheme were made known it was announced that a new board would be appointed, largely representing the financial interests involved, though C. F. Bernhard would remain Managing Director. Until the new board is announced and particulars of shareholdings registered, it is impossible to state who these interests are. The directors of the old Union Cinema Co., Ltd., were D. Bernhard (Chairman), C. F. Bernhard (Managing), also Chairman of Montague Lyon, Ltd., and Managing Director of Pointer & Co., Ltd., and of 29 cinema companies), L. J. Clements, with P. J. Davis as alternative for Clements. Apart from the Bernhards, the largest shareholders were bankers' nominee companies (particularly Branch Nominees), although the Equity & Law Life Assurance Society and the Eastern & S. African Telegraph Co. also held 30,000 and 14,500 preference shares respectively.

ODEON THEATRES, LTD.—Is a private company registered in October, 1933' with £100 capital. The latter was increased to £200,000 in March, 1935, being divided into 150,000 preference shares of £1 and 100,000 ordinary shares of 10/-. All the ordinary and 50,000 of the preference shares were taken up by June, 1936. Directors: Oscar Deutsch, F. S. Bates and W. G. Elcock (Chartered Accountant). Deutsch holds 99,800 of the issued ordinary and all the issued preference shares, Bates and Elcock holding 100 ordinary shares each. Each of the theatres controlled by the circuit is registered as a separate company, raising capital and taking up loans on its own account.

ODEON TRUST. LTD., is also a private company ; its capital is £3,000, and the directors are the same as those of Odeon Theatres, Ltd., with the addition of A. Fletcher (Solicitor) and C. E. Worthington, Leicester (Provision Merchant). The largest shareholders are C. E. Worthington, I. Polsky (Director, Odeon, S. Harrow, Ltd.) and O. Deutsch.

Neither Odeon Theatres nor Odeon Trust show any indication of a United Artist holding in their Somerset House records, but there can be no doubt of the fact of such a holding in one or other of the Deutsch companies, since it was widely reported as a statement of O. Deutsch himself in the financial and film press (the *Investors' Chronicle* of 24.10.36—leading article on Film Finance—even speaks of a 50 per cent. holding).

In November, 1936, the Odeon group of companies was increased by Cinema Ground Rents & Properties, Ltd., a new company with a nominal capital of £5,000,000 in £1 shares. The object of the concern is stated to be primarily that of acquiring new sites for Odeon cinemas. Its commitments in this direction are reported already to exceed £1,000,000. No details are as yet available concerning the shareholders of this concern, but its board consists of :

PHILIP E. HILL, Chairman, also director of :—

>Armstrong Siddeley Development Co., Ltd.
>Beechams Pills, Ltd. (Chairman).
>Covent Garden Properties Co., Ltd. (Chairman).
>Eagle, Star and British Dominions Insurance Co., Ltd.
>Hawker Siddeley Aircraft Co., Ltd.
>Olympia, Ltd. (Chairman).
>Philip Hill & Partners, Ltd. (Chairman).
>Pritchard & Constance (Manufacturing), Ltd. (Chairman).
>Quadrant Trust, Ltd.
>R. Hovenden & Sons, Ltd. (Chairman).
>Scribbans & Co., Ltd. (Chairman).
>Second Covent Garden Property Co., Ltd. (Chairman).
>Taylors (Cash Chemists), London, Ltd. (Chairman).
>Taylors (Cash Chemists) Midland Ltd. (Chairman).
>Taylors (Cash Chemists) Trust, Ltd. (Chairman).

Taylors Drug Co., Ltd. (Chairman).
Timothy Whites & Taylors, Ltd. (Chairman).
Veno Drug Co., Ltd. (Chairman).
Whites Property Co., Ltd. (Chairman).

LOUIS NICHOLAS, Managing Director, Chartered Accountant and Director of :—
Beechams Pills, Ltd. (Vice-Chairman).
Clarendon Property Co., Ltd. (Chairman).
Covent Garden Properties Co., Ltd.
Olympia, Ltd.
Philip Hill & Partners, Ltd.
Quadrant Trust, Ltd.
Scribbans & Co., Ltd.
Second Covent Garden Property Co., Ltd.
Taylor (Cash Chemists), London Ltd.
Taylors (Cash Chemists) Trust, Ltd.
Timothy Whites & Taylors, Ltd. (Vice-Chairman).
Walbrook Trust, Ltd. (Chairman).

SIR E. M. MOUNTAIN, Chairman and Managing Director of :—
Eagle, Star and British Dominions Insurance Co., Ltd.
also on the board of :—
British Crown Assurance Corporation, Ltd. (Chairman).
British North-western Fire Insurance Co., Ltd.
Covent Garden Properties Co., Ltd.
Liverpool Reversionary Co., Ltd.
Olympia, Ltd.
Premier Motor Policies. Ltd.
Second Covent Garden Properties Co., Ltd.
Threadneedle Insurance Co. (1923), Ltd. (Chairman).

HUBERT A. MEREDITH, City Editor, *Daily Mirror, Daily Mail, Evening News and Sunday Pictorial*, and director of :—
A. F. Sherley & Co., Ltd.
Beechams Pills, Ltd.
Exhibitions, Ltd.
H.P. Syndicate, Ltd.
Philip Hill & Partners, Ltd.
Phosferine (Ashton & Parsons), Ltd.
Pritchard & Constance (Manufacturing), Ltd.
Scribbans & Co., Ltd.
Veno Drug Co., Ltd.

COUNTY CINEMAS, LTD.—Registered 1927, with an authorised capital of £125,000, of which £108,707 was issued, divided into 10,000 7½ per cent, 1st preference shares of £1, 9,215 8 per cent. 2nd preference Shares of £1. and 89,492 ordinary shares of £1. There were also undischarged mortgages of £72,275. In March, 1936, a new capital issue of £1,515,000 through the London Industrial Finance Trust, Ltd., was announced, but the issue was subsequently withdrawn and it was stated that it would be placed privately. Directors : J. Amery-Parkes, also Director of Assoc. Theatre Properties (London) Ltd ; Fiat (London), Ltd. ; Gaiety Theatre Co., Ltd. ; H.M. & S., Ltd. George Gee, also Director of Gee, Walker & Slater, Ltd. ; Hunziker (Gt. Britain), Ltd.; W. D. Bartholomew, also Director of Entertainments & General Investment Corp., Ltd., Commander G. P. Lewis, G. M. J. L. Whitmore, G. Archibald, also Director of United Artists Corp., Ltd. ; C. J. Donada (Managing Director), also Director of Entertainments & General Investment Corp., Ltd.

The Entertainments & General Investment Corp., Ltd., with 75,900 ordinary shares, are the largest shareholders ; others listed are : L. P. Beever, with

1,300 2nd Pref. and 10,942 ordinary shares, and W. D. Bartholomew, with 7,050 1st preference shares.

Entertainments & General Investment Corp., Ltd ,formed in 1930 with a nominal capital of £210,000, has a board similar to that of County Cinemas, M. Silverstone of United Artists being an additional director. The bulk of its shares are held by board members of County Cinemas, Ltd., but F. M. Guedalla, of U.A., also holds a substantial blocks of ordinary shares.

The cinemas of this circuit appear also to be registered as separate companies, raising capital in their own names.

B.—Independent Production Finance.

47. The rapid expansion during the last eighteen months of British independent production on a scale more ambitious than that of mere quota " quickies," has led to a financial situation which bears all the characteristics of a highly speculative trade boom. As we have seen, these production units are almost without exception private companies, with relatively insignificant capital resources of their own. The great bulk of the production cost incurred by them is secured by means of insurance policies against the non-payment of bank overdrafts with specified limits, varying from £1,500 to £450,000 on single guarantees. The security offered is the highly problematical one of the expected returns from films about to be produced or in process of production. It should be noted that this short term loan financing is resorted to even in those cases where a percentage of the cost is advanced by the distributing concern for whom the film is being produced, while the bank overdraft of Gaumont-British shows that even the large combines, relying mainly on the assured market of their cinema circuits, are affected as soon as they attempt to produce for a world market. In order to obtain an idea of the scale of this financing and of the financial interests involved, we have made an analysis of the particulars of charges registered, as published in the *Kinematograph Weekly*, between February and November, 1936.* From this analysis it appears that the total amount raised in the form of guarantees (and in a few instances in that of debentures) by production companies, other than studio enterprises, between January 16th and October 30th, was in excess of £4,050,000 (in six instances the amount charged was unspecified). £2,823,300 of this sum represents guaranteed advances for which a single company Aldgate Trustees Ltd., acting as trustees for the unknown guarantors, is registered as " mortgagees or persons entitled to the charge."** The companies concerned and the sums were :—

---

* These particulars are not necessarily complete, and they refer exclusively to the first 10 months of 1936.

**Companies Act, 1929, Section 79 : " Particulars of mortgages or charges created by a company registered in England."

Joseph Arthur Rank, D.L., J.P.

The Lord Luke of Pavenham   The Rt. Hon. Lord Portal of Laverstoke

Herbert Wilcox

C. M. Woolf

Max Schach

John Corfield

United Artists group of producers :—	£	£
Criterion Film Prods., Ltd.	207,000	
Atlantic Film Prods., Ltd.	58,750	
Trafalgar Film Prods., Ltd.	450,000	
Soskin Film Prods., Ltd.	17,500	
Total		733,250
General Film Distributors, Ltd., group of producers :—		
Capitol Film Corp., Ltd.	1,100,000	(4 separate
Cecil Films, Ltd.	150,000	charges)
City Film Corp., Ltd.	134,650	
J. G. & R. B. Wainwright, Ltd.	12,000	
Total		1,396,650
A.B.F.D. group of producers :—		
Franco-London Films, Ltd.	25,000	
Toeplitz Productions, Ltd.	20,000	
Total		45,000
Other Producers :—		
T. A. Welch Productions, Ltd.	5,000	
John Stafford Productions, Ltd.	200,000	
Hammer Productions, Ltd.	27,000	
London Screen Plays, Ltd.	29,400	
British Artistic Films, Ltd.	17,500	
Buckingham Film Prod., Ltd.	150,000	
Mondover Film Prod., Ltd.	4,000	
Tudor Films, Ltd.	20,000	
London & Continental Films, Ltd.	22,500	
Garrick Film Co., Ltd.	22,000	
John Clein Pictures, Ltd.	27,000	
Argyle British Prod., Ltd.	9,500	
Grosvenor Sound Films, Ltd.	90,000	
Beaumont Film Prod., Ltd.	20,000	
Malcolm British Prod., Ltd.	4,500	
Total		648,400
Grand Total ...		*£2,823,300

ALDGATE TRUSTEES, LTD.—Is a private company, registered in July, 1935, with a capital of £1,000, of which £98 is paid up. The Directors are : F. C. Ells, a member of Lloyds, L. H. Wilkins, an incorporated insurance broker (both directors of Glanvill, Enthoven & Co.), S. B. Smith, a chartered accountant.

Other groups of importance in the sphere of production advances during 1936 are : Prudential Assurance Co., Ltd., which in October took up debentures for London Film Productions, C. T. Bowring & Co. (Insurance), Ltd., which took up £274,702 debentures also for London Films (October) and Denham Securities, Ltd., which guaranteed £300,000 for New World Pictures, Ltd., and £320,000 for Victor Saville Productions, Ltd., while the Equity & Law Life Assurance Society took up £160,000 debentures and collateral mortgage securities for the Capital Film Corporation, Ltd., secured on certain films and money in the joint account of Capital

---

* It should be noted, moreover, that in many cases there were prior charges outstanding against the films offered as security.

Film and Aldgate Trustees, and a further £60,000 for Trafalgar Productions, Ltd. Smaller advances were made by the Clydesdale Bank, Ltd. (Grafton Films, Ltd., £10,000), Butchers Film Service, Ltd. (Malcolm Picture Productions, Ltd., £2,540) and the Bankers Trust Co. (Fitzpatrick Pictures, Ltd., £2,000), to mention only a few instances.

The case of Capitol Film Corporation is particularly instructive. In the first place the capital resources of this company (£125,000) are above the average for independent producers. Secondly, we note from the particulars of charges filed, that at least in the case of four films 37½ per cent. of the actual cost of production was advanced by General Film Distributors. Also, the company secured through Aldgate Trustees guaranteed overdrafts with the Westminster Bank of £450,000, £360,000 and £140,000 respectively, and with the District Bank of £150,000. Nor is this all, for in addition it raised debentures and collateral mortgages for £160,000 from the Equity & Law Life Assurance Society.*

In three cases advances from individuals are indicated. Thus Alan D. Daly, of Elstree, advanced £10,000 to Tudor Films, Ltd., in July ; Capt. A. S. Cunningham-Reid advanced £5,000 to Criterion Films, Ltd., in March ; while J. R. T. Pilkington, of Dublin, and N. Clarke, London, advanced £750 to Neville Clarke Productions, Ltd.

C.—MORTGAGE AND DEBENTURE FINANCE IN THE EXHIBITION SPHERE.

48.　While the curious method of financing discussed in the last paragraph appears to be confined to the production sphere, the rapid expansion in the theatre holdings of the large and medium sized circuits to which we have already referred, is reflected in an equally marked increase in the mortgage and debenture indebtedness of cinema-owning companies. During the first ten months of 1936 no less a sum than over £7,806,642 (eight charges being unspecified was secured in the form of mortgages or debentures on cinema properties. This sum was distributed as follows :—

	£	
G.B. group	711,500*	*(excl. the £1,340,000 debenture cover for Bank overdrafts of Gaumont-British Picture Corporation Ltd.)
A.B.P.C. group ...	4,167,242†	†(incl. £3,500,000 debentures of Associated British Picture Corporation Ltd. and £592,742 deb., etc., of Ass. Cinema Properties, Ltd.)
Union group	1,300,000	NOTE.—This table is subject to correction, since cinemas in the course of construction
Odeon group, over ...	255,000	could not always be assigned with certainty
County group	641,650	to a controlling group. It should also be
Other Companies over	731,250	remembered that these figures are compiled from the reports published in the Kinema-
Total	£7,806,642	tograph Weekly and may not be entirely complete.

* Not including charges taken up in 1935.

To complete the picture of mortgage-debenture financing during the first ten months of this year, we must add over £368,000 on account of distributing concerns (Twickenham Film Distributors, Ltd., with £150,000 and Associated British Film Distributors, Ltd., with £140,000 being the largest debtors), and over £382,250 on account of studio enterprises (Pinewood Studios with £300,000 and Worton Hall Studios with £78,000 being the largest items). Adding all these items together, we find that in the first ten months of 1936 the British film industry in its three spheres of production, distribution and exhibition, took up short term loans or fixed interest bearing mortgages, etc., amounting to a sum in excess of £12,635,000.

The most prominent financial groups concerned in these loans (other than Aldgate Trustees, Denham Securities and Prudential Assurance) are :—

LAW DEBENTURE CORPORATION, LTD. :

		£
Exhibition :	Associated British Picture Corporation, Ltd. ...	3,500,000
	Gaumont-British (Gen. Theatres Corp. & Haymarket Capitol)	550,000
	Total ...	4,050,000

BRANCH NOMINEES, LTD. :

		£
Distribution :	Associated British Film Distributors, Ltd. ...	140,000
Exhibition :	A.B.P.C. Group (Ass. Cinem. Prop.)	500,000
	Odeon group...	66,000
	Union group	800,000
	County group	460,000
	Other cinema companies	60,000
	Total ...	2,026,000

EQUITY & LAW LIFE ASSURANCE SOC. :

		£
Production :	Capitol Film Corp.	160,000
	Trafalgar Film Prods.	60,000
Studios :	Pinewood Studios	300,000
Exhibition :	Union group	500,000
	County group	35,000
	Total ...	1,055,000

MORRIS MOTORS, LTD. :

		£
Exhibition :	Coliseum Syndicate (secured on Coliseum & Chandos Public House)	300,000

C. T. BOWRING & CO. (INS.), LTD. :

		£
Production :	London Film Prod., Ltd.	247,702
Distribution :	Ace Films, Ltd.	90,000
	Nat. Provinc. Film Distr., Ltd.	25,000
	Twickenham Film Distr., Ltd.	150,000
	Total ...	512,702

GUARDIAN ASSURANCE CO., LTD. :

		£
Exhibition :	Gaumont Super Cinemas, Ltd.	140,000

EAGLE, STAR AND BRITISH DOMINIONS INSURANCE CO., LTD. :

		£
Exhibition :	Odeon Theatres	100,400
	Palace (Chatham), Ltd.	22,800
	Total ...	123,200

NORWICH UNION LIFE INS. SOC., LTD. :
    Exhibition :   Majestic Theatre Corp.   90,000

ATLAS ASSURANCE CO., LTD.:
    Exhibition :   Associated British Picture Corporation sub-
             sidiaries   75,000

Other companies engaged in cinema loans include :
    Halifax Building Soc. (Twentieth Cent. Cinem. & Paramount
        Picture Theatres) ...   .   69,000 (and further advances)
    Cinema Realisations (Liverpool), Ltd. (Associated British
        Picture Corporation Group)   47,500
    Brocklyn Trust (Manchester) (Odeon)   35,650
    Westminster Perm. Bldg. Soc. (Odeon)   18,450
    Leightons (Contractors), Ltd. (Odeon)   ...   20% of build. contr. price.
    Gleniffer Properties (County)   24,000
    Entertainments & Gen. Inv. Co. (County)   4,000

Individual creditors range from O. Daniels, of Hyde, who advanced £500 to Northern Amusements, Ltd., to S. W. Gibbons, Nottingham, who advanced £80,000 to the Ritz (Nottingham), Ltd. (County group), and include :—

    J. Rothstein, London (Ass. Cinem. Props.)   31,000
    R. Shapiro & G. A. Saunders, London (Gaum. Super Cin.)   ...   11,500
    L. D. Woolfe, London (Odeon)   5,000
    J. Milner, London (Odeon)   11,000
    Mrs. R. King, Nottingham (Adelphi Entertainments)   6,000
    A. E. Thompson, Farnham, and others (Ass. Cin. Prop.)   ...   5,000
    Maj. T. G. F. Paget and J. W. Paget (West Cliff Gard. Theatre)
        Clacton   4,000

In a certain number of cases, mortgages and similar loans are apparently taken up by various banks in their own names. In the majority of instances the amount involved is not disclosed, but the banks in question and their debtors are as follows :—

Lloyds Bank :   Worthing Hall & Winter Garden £70,000.
                     Clifton Cinema (Leominster), Ltd., £10,000.
                     Clifton Picture House (York), Ltd., " all money due ", etc
                     Seaford Empire, Co., Ltd., " all money due ", etc.
Wm. Deacons Bank :   Kenyons Playhouses, Ltd., £50,000.
Barclays Bank :   Hinge's Cinemas, Ltd., £20,000.
                     Majestic (Sevenoaks), Ltd., " all money due ", etc.
                     Princess Cinema (Bagshot) Ltd., " all money due ", etc.
                     Pinewood Studios, " all money due ", etc.
                     Milheath Studios, " all money due ", etc.
Union Bank (Manchester) Odeon (Guide Bridge), Ltd., £12,000.
Midland Bank :   Twentieth Century Cinemas, " all money due ", etc.
                     Fox British Pictures (Studio), " all money due ", etc.
                     Inc. Assoc. of Kinematograph Manufacturers, " all money
                         due ", etc.
Clydesdale Bank :   Grafton Films, Ltd., £10,000.

III.—FINANCE (CONCLUSIONS.)

49. (a) *The Present Phase of British Film Finance.* With its tempestuous expansion and curious financing, the present phase in the development of the British film industry has all the appearance of a hectic boom rushing towards its culmination point. But it is a boom that has a number of peculiar features. We shall endeavour in this section briefly to indicate (a) the tempo of present expansion, (b) the most striking of the features that distinguish the film boom from similar experiences elsewhere.

The expansion of the trade is reflected in the figures for new companies registered. Taking the particulars published in the *Kinematograph Weekly* and *Kinematograph Yearbook* respectively, we find that during the last twelve years, new film, cinema, etc., companies were registered at the following rate :—

YEAR	PRODUCTION*	RENTING	EXHIBITION	MISCELLANOUS. (including Equipment, etc.)	TOTAL.
1925	15	25	110	26	176
1926	21	25	138	26	210
1927	26	17	143	29	215
1928	37	16	94	25	172
1929	59	3	150	58	270
1930	36	4	176	48	264
1931	55	5	174	49	283
1932	46	7	212	38	303
1933	64	6	222	57	349
1934	86	10	251	68	415
1935	108	13	226	64	411
1936 (10 mths.)	87	7	196	47	337

The rate of acceleration so clearly marked particularly in the production companies' figures, is even more accentuatedly reflected in the following figures kindly supplied by Messrs. Jordan & Sons, Ltd. (the totals differ from those of the preceding series owing to certain differences of classification) :—

Number of new Film and Cinema Companies and their total nominal capital registered in 1931-36 :—

YEAR.	NO. OF COMPANIES.	TOTAL CAPITAL (£).
1931	201	972,600
1932	224	1,344,509
1933	253	2,258,290
1934	259	1,895;435
1935	338	3,677,440
1936	395	15,921,565**

It will be seen from both these series that the expansion which commences in about 1933, became most marked in 1935 (and in the first months of 1936), but in view of the necessary time lag between the registration of a company and the actual completion of its first

---

* Including a small proportion of renter-producers.

**Including Cinema Ground Rents and Properties, Ltd., with £5,000,000 capital which is classified as a land company by Messrs. Jordan & Sons, Ltd. The other main companies in the 1936 total are Union Cinemas, Ltd. with £6,500,000 and G. C. F. Corporation, Ltd. with £1,225,000 capital.

production or of its new cinema, we have only in recent months commenced to feel the effects of this development.

One of the most striking features of this expansion from a financial point of view, is the fact that on the production side it is based almost entirely on *expectation* without any concrete results to justify that optimism, for the older companies that confine their activities to production, or production and renting, have for a number of years not been showing any substantial profits. By the time the first products of the new enterprises actually reach the market and the optimistic expectations can be tested, the first signs of an abatement in the forward movement can already be detected.

The second peculiar feature which applies to all branches of the industry, is that the expansion has with few outstanding exceptions been financed not by increases in the companies' own working capital, but by a spectacular increase in *loans* (whereas in " normal " booms the actual increase in business usually enables the expanding enterprises largely to liquidate existing loan obligations).

In paragraphs 47 and 48, we have indicated the extent to which both short and long term loans have been taken up by all branches of the industry, even within so brief a period as the first ten months of 1936, but there is reason to believe that it is this period and the latter half of 1935, which saw the most decisive increase in the industry's indebtedness. The following summary attempts to indicate the ratio between capital and loans in the two great combines and in the new production units (for the exhibition sphere this comparison is very difficult in view of the fact that even in most of the large circuits, each cinema has a separate corporate existence, with separate capital and indebtedness) :—

	CAPITAL	DEBENTURES MORTGAGES OR SHORT TERM CREDITS
	£	£
COMBINES :		
Gaumont-British Picture Corporation, Ltd. ...	6,250,000	6,500,000
Associated British Picture Corporation, Ltd. ...	3,550,000	3,500,000
	9,800,000	10,000,000
PRODUCTION AND RENTING COMPANIES :		
Old Production Units*	1,413,500	428,000
New Studio and Distributing Units**	1,670,000	378,000
New Production Units***	1,035,000	4,229,000
(State of October, 1936.)	4,118,500	5,035,000

* British and Dominion Films, A.T.P., Stoll, Sound City, Twickenham Studios, British Lion.
** G.C.F. Corporation, General Film Distributors, Pinewood Studios, Worton Hall Studios.
*** London Film Productions, Criterion Films, British Cine Alliance, Pall Mall, Trafalgar, V. Saville, Atlantic Films, British Pictorial Productions, British National Films, City Films, H. Wilcox, Capitol Film Corporation, Cecil, Toeplitz, Rock, Fuller, Grosvenor, Hammer.

However fragmentary these figures may be, the fact of the ever ncreasing weight of loan money as distinct from shareholders' capital emerges incontestably, even for the large corporations, while in the case of the new production units, the superiority of the former is overwhelming. Most of the latter units are in fact little more than the executive agents of their creditors (the facts are even more striking than the figures suggest, since the latter are weighted towards the capital side by one or two units such as British National or Toeplitz having relatively large capital with little or no loans).

Nor is this all, for an analysis of earnings, in so far as these are published, shows that where there are any profits in the production and distribution sphere, these are not, on the whole, benefiting the ordinary shareholders, but the fixed interest bearing security holders. And this is particularly true of the old production units, where the shareholders' capital greatly exceeds the loan capital. In the cinema sphere, on the other hand, it appears that even the ordinary shareholders are getting dividends at present :—

DIVIDENDS PAID ON ORDINARY SHARES, 1933-1936 (%)

	1933	1934	1935	1936
PRODUCTION AND EXHIBITION				
Gaumont-British Picture Corporation Ltd.	7	7	7	Nil
Associated British Picture Corporation Ltd.	5	6	10	12½
PRODUCTION				
British and Dominion Films, Ltd. ...		8*	Nil	Nil
British Lion	Nil	Nil	Nil	Nil
A.T.P.	Nil	Nil	Nil	Nil
Sound City	...(made public Co., 1935)			3
EXHIBITION				
Union	6	10	20 & 5	22 & 5
P.C.T.	15	15	15	15

There thus arises the curious situation that at least in one of the spheres most affected by expansion (production) the ordinary shareholders are not making any money even in the boom period.

The final characteristic of the present phase is one which the film trade has in common with other industries : the trend to ever greater concentration. In this process the relative increase of loan money is one of the most powerful agents, for the credits obtained by the various production or exhibition units tend to an increasing extent to emanate from a few powerful financial groups, who thus obtain a degree of control overriding the competitive barriers within the industry.

---

* For eighteen months, 1933-4.

50. (b) *The Men Behind the Movies.* The extent to which the
men behind the movies in the renting and production, and recently
also in the exhibition sphere, are the controllers of the great American
film groups, has already been discussed at length. Turning to
British interests proper, we find that the unification of ultimate
control which is so striking a feature of the American film industry,
is not as yet found to the same extent in the British movie trade, the
position of which is from this point of view in many respects similar
to that of the American industry about 1927/8, prior to the crisis and
the introduction of sound. That is to say that, while there is still a
great deal of decentralisation, the lines along which unification will be
achieved and the groups which are preparing to take control as soon
as a crash or some other cause provides them with a chance to do so,
can already be roughly perceived through the mist of nominee companies, finance agencies and the corporate facades of *ad hoc* syndi-
cates. One of the features in the company flotation position peculiar
to 1936 is the sudden and startling increase in the number of new
film financing companies registered, which leapt up from one
in 1935 to seventeen in the first 10 months of 1936. Among these
groups foreign interests have not been entirely lacking. Thus we
find that the principal figure behind the General Film Finance,
Ltd., registered in August, 1936, is Lawrence Fox, described as an
American banker who intends to create a new organisation for the
production of films in England. And there was also a mysterious
report, somewhat sinister in its political implications, in the
Evening Standard of 17.9.36, according to which representatives
of German financiers were sounding opinion in the City concerning a
scheme " to establish in this country an organisation similar to the
German film bank which finances German films." The bank would
advance resources for the production of films, the character of which
it approves. Nothing appears to have come of these plans.

The dominating interests among the directors and shareholders
(in so far as their identity is not concealed behind bankers nominee
companies) of the great English and Anglo-American renting concerns have already been indicated in paragraphs 23—45. Among
them the Rank-Portal (G.F.D.), and the Prudential — Bowring
—Warburg (Korda) groups loom as the most powerful interests
next to the Chase National Bank—Balfour, Broadman—Fox
interests in Gaumont-British Picture Corporation, Ltd. Of
equal importance for the future control of the industry are
probably the most influential among the debenture and mortgage
holding concerns listed in paragraph 48.

Through its position as trustee for all the Associated British
Picture Corporation, Ltd., debentures as well as for many debentures
of Gaumont-British subsidiaries, the Law Debenture Corporation,
Ltd., deserves first place as creditor of the movie industry. Its chairman, Sir Miles W. Mattinson, K.C., is at the same time chairman of

Ellerman Lines, Ltd., the main shipping company among the concerns controlled by youthful Sir John Ellerman, heir to the £36,685,000 estate left by his father a few years ago. Both Sir Miles Mattinson and W. Graham are also directors of several other Ellerman companies, while in addition the latter is chairman of Bisichi Tin Co (Nigeria), Ltd., and Illustrated London News & Sketch, Ltd., Illustrated Sporting & Dramatic Publishing Co., Ltd., etc., and director of Associated Tin Mines of Nigeria, Ltd., River Plate Electricity Co., Ltd., etc. Lord Greenwood combines his Law Debenture Corporation directorship with other director-ships in heavy industry (Dorman, Long & Co., etc.), food (Aerated Bread Co.), tailoring (Montague Burton), insurance (Phœnix Assurance), coal (Upton Colliery) and electricity (Soc. Internat. d'Energie Hydro Electrique). Its other directors are Bernard Campion, K.C., Sir Francis Fladgate, M.V.O. (Phœnix Assur-ance and four electricity companies in London), R. L. Hunter (Meux Brewery and Guardian Assurance) and J. H. C. Johnston (Cordoba Central Railway Co. and numerous investment companies).

Next perhaps in importance is the National Provincial Bank, Ltd., with its overdraft facilities for Gaumont-British Picture Corporation, Ltd., converted into £1,340,000 debentures, an over-draft of £163,403 to A.T.P., and as the parent institution of the bankers nominee company (Branch Nominees, Ltd.) having perhaps the largest share and mortgage, etc., holdings in the industry (Associated British Picture Corporation, Ltd., Associated British Film Distributors, Ltd., Union, County, Odeon, etc.). Although the control of investments registered in the name of nominee com-panies is stated to rest entirely with the clients for whom they are made and not with the parent bank, it is nevertheless interesting that the nominee company most prominently involved in the film trade is associated with that among the great commercial banks which appears to have granted by far the largest credits in its own name to the industry. The directors of the National Provincial bank are :—

Chairman : C. F. Campbell.
Deputy- : F. A. Johnston.
Chairmen Sir A. E. Lewis.

Directors:
Lord Burghley, M.P.
Sir Harcourt Butler.
Colin Cooper.
J. C. D. Denison-Pender.
C. G. Hamilton.
C. F. Hotblack.
Lord Illingworth.
Sir John B. Lloyd.

Directors:
Sir Austin Low.
Ronald Malcolm.
Sir Percival L. D. Perry.
Hon. Jasper N. Ridley.
Lord Riverdale.
John Robarts.
Sir Samuel Roberts, Bt.
E. A. Smith.
Capt. E. C. E. Smith.

Third in the list of film creditors is the Equity & Law Life Assurance Society, whose interests cover all three spheres of the trade (Capitol Film Corporation, Pinewood Studios, Union, County, etc. ; the prominence of the legal investment or insurance concerns is a curious feature of present-day film finance). The directors of this prospering concern, paying dividends ranging from 25 to 35 per cent. per annum on its ordinary shares (since 1925) are :—

Chairman : Rt. Hon. Sir Dennis H. Herbert, K.B.E., M.P.

Deputy-Chairman : Sir Bernhard E. H. Bircham.

Directors
- H. M. Crookenden.
- Lord Ernle.
- H. M. Farrer.
- Sir Roger Gregory.
- R. F. Holme.
- A. H. James.
- Lord Kennet.
- Rt. Hon. C. A. McCurdy.
- A. E. Messer.
- W. P. Phelps.
- Sir Roger Poole.
- C. Wigan.

We have already encountered R. F. Holme as a director of Radio Pictures, Ltd. and Radio-Keith Orpheum, Ltd. Rt. Hon. C. A. McCurdy is also a director of London Express Newspaper, Ltd., while A. E. Messer is interested in Trinidad Lake Asphalt, Iboro Sugar Estates, etc. The other interests of this group, as revealed in their directorships are mainly confined to the investment and insurance spheres.

Like the Warburg banks, the Bowring companies, comprising an old established merchant house in Liverpool, Newfoundland and the United States, a shipping enterprise and associated finance and insurance undertakings, are almost wholly family concerns. The Bowring family are the descendants of an early 17th century Devonshire woollen weaver, and their prosperity dates mainly from the establishment of their Newfoundland business in the early 19th century. The present heads of C. T. Bowring & Co., Ltd., are Sir F. C. Bowring, J.P. (chairman) and Hon. Sir Edgar R. Bowring, K.C.M.G.

In the Prudential Assurance Co., Ltd., whose total assets exceed £302 million, we meet one of the most powerful financial organisations of the modern capitalist world. Built up on the weekly penny premium payments of some 27¼ million working class households in this country, the interests of this concern, established by means of cross-directorships, investments and loans, extend from the United States to India, from the British Mutual Banking Co., Ltd., to Marks and Spencers, from German government loans and British armament makers to London films. The following twelve men are the directors of this concern :—

Chairman : Sir Edgar Horne.
Deputy-Chairman : Frederick Schooling.
    ,,   ,,   Sir George S. Barstow.

Directors
- A. R. Barrand.
- Sir Laurence N. Guillemard.
- G. P. Harben.
- Major William Guy Horne.
- J. R. Lancaster.
- Sir John H. Luscombe.
- Lt.-Col. P. L. Reid.
- Ernest Dewey.
- H. H. Moseley.

We are left in conclusion with the question of the Aldgate Trustees, Ltd. This is a trustee company. The interests on whose behalf it works are not known. But in view of its important position in British film finance—it is registered as the trustees for charges totalling over £3,000,000 taken up during 1935/36—it is of interest to state what facts are known about this firm. One will remember that in dealing with the Pinewood Studios, Ltd. —which is the studio concern closely associated with the Rank-Portal-Lindenburg-Farrow-Luke group of companies—we found that a certain Mr. Harold Godfrey Judd was one of the board members. Already, as we have seen, this group has emerged, during the last eighteen months, as a very powerful factor. It controls one of the most important renting concerns, has connections with one of the eight major American producer-renter companies, is connected with a great new studio enterprise and is building up a rapidly expanding cinema circuit. It is therefore of interest to note the following facts :—*

(1) One of the film companies for whom Aldgate Trustees, Ltd., secured advances in 1935 was New Ideal Pictures Ltd. (charges of £65,000). On 18th February, 1936, the Aldgate Trustees, Ltd., gave notice of the appointment by them, on 30th January, 1936, of Harold Godfrey Judd, of 8, Fredericks Place, E.C.2, as receiver and manager for New Ideal Pictures, Ltd.

(2) The Company Registration Department File No. 300422 for Twickenham Film Distributors, Ltd., contains the following entry : Deed of Charge, dated 30th October, 1936, to secure Balance of £35,000 remaining due under the Heads of an Agreement dated 26th March, 1936, between (1) Harold Godfrey Judd (Recr.), (2) Frank Charles Ells

---

*The list of Mr. H. G. Judd's directorships (page 40) also includes the firm of lead merchants, H. J. Enthoven and Sons, Ltd., while both Mr. F. C. Ells and Mr. L. H. Wilkins are partners of the insurance firm of Glanvill, Enthoven and Co. Another partner of this latter firm is Mr. Frederick Vernon Enthoven, who is also a shareholder in H. J. Enthoven and Sons, Ltd. We are, however, informed that H. J. Enthoven and Sons, Ltd., are in no way concerned in the activities of Aldgate Trustees, Ltd.

and Leopold Howard Wilkins, (3) Aldgate Trustees, Ltd., (4) the Company, and Supplemental Agreement, dated 29th October, 1936, between the same parties in respect of certain films sold to the Company . . . (a list of films is specified which are to serve as security, subject to certain conditions) . . . Mortgagee or Person entitled to the Charge :   Harold Godfrey Judd, 8, Fredericks Place, E.C.2.

December, 1936

APPENDIX
A SUMMARY HISTORY OF AMERICAN FILM FINANCE.

In view of the important position of the American film companies in the British cinema industry no account of the latter would be complete without at least a summary statement of American film finance. For this reason we are reprinting in the form of an appendix a Film Council report on this subject first published with some abbreviations in the *World Film News* of November, 1936.

CONTENTS

THE PRESENT STRUCTURE OF THE AMERICAN FILM INDUSTRY

The American Film Industry was estimated in 1935-6 to represent an investment of some $2,000,000,000. It catered for the entertainment of weekly audiences numbering 80 to 85,000,000 in the United States alone. Paramount Pictures Inc., Warner Bros. Pictures Inc., Twentieth Century-Fox Film Corp., Loew's Inc. (controlling Metro-Goldwyn-Mayer), Radio-Keith-Orpheum Corp., Universal Corp., Columbia Pictures Corp., and United Artists Corp., are the eight major companies dominating this industry, the present structure of which is summarised in Table I. We shall endeavour in the following pages to give a brief account of the manner in which the companies listed attained their present controlling position and of the financial interests they represent.

STRUCTURE OF THE AMERICAN FILM INDUSTRY 1935-6.
(SOURCES : N.R.A. REPORT AND MOTION PICTURE ALMANAC, 1936-7)

PRODUCTION.

EIGHT MAJOR COMPANIES CONTROL :

80% of the capital invested in production ;
65% of feature film output as measured by No. of films ;
80% of feature film output as measured by COST of films ;
100% of the news film services.

33 MINOR PRODUCERS were sufficiently important to be listed in the Motion Picture Almanac, 1935-6.

100-200 SMALL PRODUCERS released occasional films.

DISTRIBUTION.

Eight National Organisations were affiliated to the eight major producing companies.

Three Independent National distributing organisations handled independent product.

Eighty-six Distributing Organisations (National and Regional), listed in the "Film Daily Yearbook, 1935," operated about 550 local film exchanges, of these 450 were affiliated to producing companies.

EXHIBITION.

CIRCUITS AFFILIATED TO THE EIGHT MAJOR COMPANIES.		UNAFFILIATED CIRCUITS.		INDEPENDENT CINEMAS.	
A. Number of Cinemas					
	No.	%	No.	%	No.	%
1936	2,192	11.8	3,464	18.7	12,852	69.5
1935	2,073	11.5	3,070	16.7	13,120	71.8
B. Seating Capacity					
	'000 seats	%	'000 seats	%	'000 seats	%
1936	2,908	25.8	2,767	24.6	5,633	49.6
1935	2,719	24.4	2,539	22.8	5,874	52.8
C. Average Number of Seats per Cinema					
1935	1,300		850		450	

The Eight Major Companies control approximately :
25% of the most desirable seating capacity ;
12% of the total number of theatres ;
100% of the First Run Theatres and many of the best second run theatres.

NOTE : The actual strength of the circuits is understated by these figures, which include all cinemas, whether open or not. In 1936 as many as 3,130 halls were in fact closed, representing 16.9 per cent. of the total (as compared with

5,895 or 30.5 per cent. in 1933). That the majority of these halls are small ones, is shown by the fact that the 16.9 per cent. closed houses included only 10.7 per cent. of the total seating capacity.

A BRIEF HISTORY OF THE AMERICAN FILM INDUSTRY

THE FIRST PHASE, 1908-12.

The period lasting approximately from 1896 to 1908 constitutes the pre-history of the American movie industry. It was an era of primæval chaos, marked by the mushroom-growth of "nickelodeons" in all parts of the country and by the frantic efforts of the Edison interests to protect and of all other production groups to pirate the basic camera and projector patents controlled by the former.

With the formation of the Motion Picture Patents Company in January, 1909, the history of American film finance on a large scale can be said to have commenced. That company, sponsored by George Kleine, the leading importer of foreign films and equipment, was a combine of the nine most important manufacturers then existing, including the Edison, Vitagraph and Biograph companies, and of the Kleine firm. All these enterprises agreed to pool their numerous patent rights (most of them having made important additions to the original Edison patents) and to acknowledge the priority of the basic Edison rights, paying royalties for their use. Licences for all these patents were issued to all the members of the combine, but strictly withheld from all other producers and equipment manufacturers. By forming the General Film Company (the first national distributing organisation in the country) during the following year, this powerful monopoly rapidly obtained complete control of the distribution sphere, absorbing 57 out of the 58 film exchanges then existing. In addition, the company attempted to enforce the complete exclusion of all films except their own from the American screens. They issued licences, against a weekly $2 fee, for the use of their projectors to all cinemas and threatened to prosecute under the patent laws any exhibitor who used the company's projectors to display films made by outsiders. Finally, the trust made a contract with the Eastman Kodak Company, according to which the latter agreed to supply film base only to the firms who were members of the pool. Fears of an anti-trust prosecution however, led to the abandonment of this monopoly arrangement in 1911.

The trust immediately proceeded to standardise the whole business of producing and distributing films by confining themselves exclusively to the production of the one- or two-reel shorts in vogue when the merger was formed and by charging uniform rentals for standard programmes composed of such films. The stranglehold of this monopoly, protected by the patent laws and

J. P. Morgan

A. H. Giannini

John D. Rockefeller

Cheever Cowdin

paying tribute to the electrical industry, thus appeared complete and the astonishing history of its breakdown provides one of the most instructive chapters in the story of modern finance.

The formation of the trust naturally aroused the violent opposition of all producers, manufacturers and distributors excluded from its benefits, and the exhibitors as a whole felt an equally natural resentment against the restrictions imposed by the combine on their choice of programmes and against the enforced $2 licence levy. It is a remarkable fact that, almost without exception, the founders of the concerns later fused in the eight major companies of to-day were in the vanguard of the struggle against the monopoly. Prominent among these independents were Carl Laemmle and R. H. Cochrane, the late and the present head of Universal, whose Independent Picture Co. (known as the " Imp ") gave rise to the star system, when they made the experiment of indicating the name of an actress on the film. The actress in question was Mary Pickford, and the star system was destined to revolutionise the industry. Of equal importance were the efforts of Adolph Zukor and W. W. Hodgkinson, founders of concerns later merged in Paramount, to introduce full-length feature films. They first attempted to persuade the trust of the advantages of this policy, only starting as independents, when their suggestions were rejected.

Foremost among the exhibitors fighting the trust was William Fox and the methods adopted by the combine to oust him are characteristic of the manner in which the struggle was conducted. One of Fox's projectionists was bribed by the trust men to take the films rented for exhibition from them nightly after the show to a house of prostitution in Hoboken. Shortly afterwards Fox's license was cancelled on the grounds that he had allowed the companies' films to be used for immoral purposes.

Fox was able, however, to defeat this ruse and the action for damages which he subsequently brought against the trust under the Sherman laws was followed by similar actions brought by innumerable other exhibitors. At the same time the combine were unable to suppress the continued pirating of their patent rights by independent producers, whose activities even before and during the existence of the merger were largely responsible for the selection of Los Angeles as the ultimate centre of the movie industry. This city being within easy reach of the Mexican border, it was a simple matter for the pirates to escape with their cameras to safety on the approach of the process servers and thugs hired by the enraged patent owners to smash up their equipment.

The overwhelming success of the feature film and star system experiments initiated by the independents and the actions brought by the exhibitors had already undermined the monopoly hold of the combine by about 1912. It received its final blow when the

General Film Company was dissolved by court order in 1915 and when the Supreme Court declared in 1917 that the purchaser of a patented projector could not be legally forced to exhibit only the manufacturer's own films.

The first film combine thus collapsed, in spite of its apparently inassailable strength, because it attempted to stabilise a new and entirely unprecedented form of mass entertainment at a time when the demand for that entertainment had only just been aroused and the lines of its future development were as yet wholly obscure. Lacking the great advantage of their opponents, who were not only of the people but also in continuous contact with the people, the executives of the combine failed to recognise the decisive importance of ever changing mass tastes entirely beyond the scope of ordinary rationalisation practices. In calling a halt they soon lagged behind the rapidly expanding requirements of their audiences, nd despite their financial and organisational supremacy, they left the field to their opponents whose main strength lay in their ability to anticipate, instead of smothering, every new desire of the movie public.

THE SECOND PHASE, 1912–1929.

The period commencing with the gradual eclipse of the patents monopoly and terminating with the general installation of sound equipment about 1929 and the impact of the crisis on the film industry during the following year constitutes the second phase in the history of American film finance. Its salient feature from the creative point of view was the emergence of the modern entertainments film of the pre-talkie era with its as yet largely undifferentiated general " human " appeals of sex, adventure, self-improvement, lavish settings, glamorous fashions and happy endings. From the organisational point of view this period saw the gradual consolidation, after incessant and bitter rivalry and many failures, of the eight major companies which dominate the industry to-day. These companies survived largely because they succeeded in breaking through the original isolation of the three distinct spheres of the industry : because as producers they secured a sufficiently widespread exhibition outlet for their films through the control of cinema circuits, or else, because as exhibitors and distributors they assured themselves of steady supplies at remunerative rentals by absorbing production units.

The Paramount organisation (a merger of Zukor's Famous Players with Lasky's and other production units that jointly absorbed the Paramount distributing organisation founded by Hodgkinson and ultimately—in 1930—controlled 1,600 cinemas in the U.S.A.) is the outstanding example of the former type. Among the exhibitors, Loew's Inc., during the lifetime of its founder always closely allied (by family ties and personal friendship) to Zukor's group, established itself in production by the absorption first of the Metro and later of the Goldwyn and Mayer units ; Fox, while expanding his theatre holdings entered production at a very early period and soon became one of the largest producers ; First National Distributors, now absorbed by Warner Bros., commenced as a defensive alliance of leading exhibitors against the encroachments of Paramount and, having established a country-wide distributing organisation, first contracted with independent producers for the supply of feature films, and later established studios of their own. The prolonged struggle between Paramount and First National was probably the most dramatic aspect of the industry during this phase of its history. Organised in 1917 in reply to Paramount's block-booking policy and high rentals, the First National was controlled by the executives of some twenty-seven powerful theatre circuits who extended their influence by granting sub-franchises for the films distributed by them to other cinema proprietors. During 1919-21 their organisation embraced some 3,400 theatres in all parts of the country. In the production sphere, they actively attracted stars from their rival, even inducing Mary Pickford to leave Zukor at a time when she was at the height of her fame. Zukor was, however, able to meet this menace by production on a De Mille scale, while in the exhibition sphere, he met his opponents on their own ground with a ruthless cinema acquisition campaign. He succeeded in acquiring controlling interests in the circuits of several of the First National shareholders themselves and was thus able to work against his rivals from within their own ranks. Only a Federal anti-trust prosecution prevented Zukor from absorbing First National. But while this prosecution—as is invariably the case drawn over many years—caused him to alter his tactics, it did not affect the substance of his policy. It was the object of the prosecution to force Zukor to confine himself to either the production or the exhibition side of the film business. By making a formal separation of these two sides of his enterprises and organising each as a separate company, Zukor prepared himself to satisfy the letter of the law (although when the case was finally decided this demand had been abandoned). At the same time, however, Zukor contin- ued the expansion policy with renewed vigour. First National received its final blow with the absorption by Zukor of its largest remaining circuit, the Katz-Balaban group. Samuel Katz, the head of this group was placed in charge of the Publix Corporation in which Zukor had merged all his theatre interests and a few years later First National lost their independence by the absorption of their last stronghold, the Stanley group, by Warner Bros. (1929).

  It was this latter move that placed Warner Bros. among the leading companies in the industry. Their position had for a long time been a precarious one, until with Fox they acted as the pioneers for the introduction of sound (at first sound on disc) from 1925-6 onwards. Even after the overwhelming success of their first full-length sound films and especially of Al Jolson's " Jazz Singer " (1927) they were seriously hampered by their lack of national exhibition facilities until their position was remedied by their control of First National.

Among the other companies R.-K.-O. was organised under the auspices of the Radio Corporation of America. at the end of our period (1928) as a merger of several production and exhibition interests, including the American Pathé unit. Universal and Columbia for a long time confined their activities to the supply of low cost features, with a few special efforts annually to act as their publicity front. Universal's theatre acquisition policy was mainly restricted to the lesser "neighbourhood" halls, while Columbia entirely refrained from this field. Lastly, United Artists arose as the distributing organisation of a number of independent producers and stars, too expensive for any of the large companies to maintain on their permanent payrolls.

From the financial point of view this phase is marked by the entry of Wall Street interests into the film world. The policy of financing their enterprises from their own profits which had sufficed for the earlier stages of the industry's development, proved inadequate in face of the vast new capital demands arising from the incomparably more expensive star-feature films and the theatre acquisition campaigns of the post-war years.

The Famous Players-Lasky group (Paramount), were the first to enlist the support of a Wall Street banking firm (in 1919) and until their last reorganisation, Kuhn Loeb & Co., acted as their main banking affiliation. Within a few years Loew, Pathé and Fox shares were listed on the New York Stock Exchange and by 1924 the securities of a dozen movie corporations were handled by Wall Street bankers. William Fox at first employed the services of the John F. Dryden-Prudential Life Insurance group, later changing over to Halsey Stuart & Co., while the Roxy Cinema, a New York hall he acquired immediately after its construction, had been financed by S. W. Straus & Co.

Warner Bros. obtained the support of the Los Angeles banker, M. H. Flint for their earliest sound experiments, and through Flint's recommendation, they soon afterwards secured the backing of the Wall Street firm Goldman, Sachs & Co., who with Hayden, Stone & Co. remained their chief bankers until the crisis. The latter banking firm had entered the movie field as supporters of First National, one of their partners having been one of the chief figures behind a move to convert First National into a closely knit merger during the final stages of their struggle with Paramount.

Loew's chief banking affiliation was Dillon, Read & Co., one of whose representatives appears still to hold a position on the

Loew board. Shields & Co and S. W. Straus & Co., were the bankers of Universal, while the San Francisco banker, A. H. Giannini still an important figure in movie finance, had close relations with W. G. McAdoo, J. Schenck and other United Artist executives, as well as with C. De Mille, Columbia and several smaller companies. Other financiers prominent in the industry during this phase were : J. Kennedy, a Boston banker, allied with one of the concerns later merged in R.K.O. ; J. Millbank, a wealthy capitalist allied with the Chase National Bank, Blair & Co., Southern Railway and similar concerns, who supported the independent activities of W. W. Hodgkinson after the latter's departure from Paramount ; and F. J. Godsol, who at one time brought the support of the Dupont interests to S. Goldwyn's enterprises.

The entry of Randolph Hearst into the film industry also dates from this phase. He established his news reel service soon after the eclipse of the Patents Trust and owned various production units for shorts and feature films which were in course of time consolidated in his " Cosmopolitan Pictures " company. While the films of the latter unit were distributed first through Paramount and later through Metro-Goldwyn-Mayer, the Hearst news service was at various times associated with Metro-Goldwyn-Mayer, Fox and Universal. Hearst also acquired control of a few picture houses.

We may summarise the financial developments of this phase by stating that after an initial move towards decentralisation, when the industry emerged from the clutches of the patents trust, the foundations were laid for its concentration on a much higher plane. After releasing the undreamed of possibilities for the development of the film as a popular form of entertainment, the eight major companies slowly emerged as powerful groups controlling the most important positions in all the three spheres of the industry and intimately linked with prominent Wall Street banking interests. It is important to note, moreover, that towards the end of our period all the pioneer film executives, except W. Fox and C. Laemmle, had allowed the financial control of their enterprises to slip out of their hands into those of their backers. As yet, however, the latter were in the main recruited from the leading investment and merchant banking houses and did not include, except indirectly, the peak figures in the American financial oligarchy.

THE THIRD PHASE, SINCE ABOUT 1929.

The present and third phase of American film finance was heralded by two consecutive and closely related events of the first magnitude. It opened with the general adoption of sound, a technical revolution that not merely transformed the whole nature of film production but also proved to have so unexpectedly stimulating an effect on the box office that for a considerable time it was

CHART 1.
INDIRECT DEPENDENCE THROUGH SOUND EQUIPMENT CONTROL

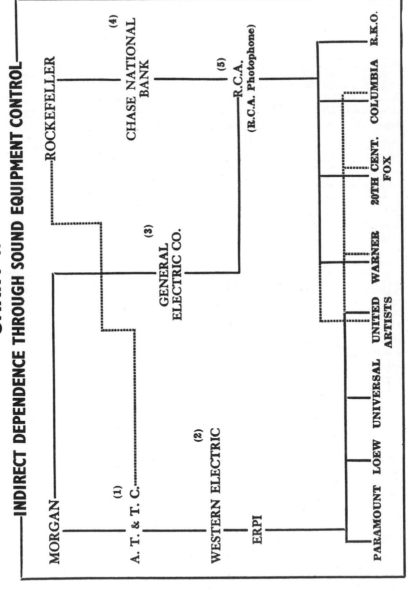

MORGAN

(1)
A. T. & T. C.

(2)
WESTERN ELECTRIC

ERPI

ROCKEFELLER

(4)
CHASE NATIONAL BANK

(5)
R.C.A.
(R.C.A. Photophone)

(3)
GENERAL ELECTRIC CO.

PARAMOUNT   LOEW   UNIVERSAL   UNITED ARTISTS   WARNER   20TH CENT. FOX   COLUMBIA   R.K.O.

able to delay the impact of the crisis, then in its first violent phase, on the film industry. The second event was the crisis itself which was rendered so much the more violent, when at last it did affect the movies, by the enormous cost involved in scrapping perfectly good equipment and product and replacing it by even more expensive new installations as a result of the technical change just indicated.

In their joint effects these two sets of events revolutionised the financial no less than the technical basis of the American movie industry. The adoption of sound led to the emergence—after violent

---

EXPLANATORY NOTES FOR CHART I.

The Morgan group (J. P. Morgan & Co., and Drexel & Co.) is the most powerful financial group in the U.S.A. to-day. Its power, built up through international and investment banking extends to every sphere of American economy. In January, 1932, Morgan partners were represented on some 35 banks and 60 non-financial corporations with assets totalling about $30 billion. Morgan influence is calculated to extend, directly or indirectly, to one quarter of the total corporate wealth of the U.S.A.

While the private wealth of the Rockefellers is even greater than that of the Morgans, their economic power, as expressed in the *control* of wealth, is not as great. Rockefeller power was built up on oil, though it now extends to many other spheres, including banking. Apart from their vast real estate holdings, Rockefeller interests appear to predominate in banks and other corporations with assets totalling about $21.5 billion (Jan., 1932).

1. AMERICAN TELEPHONE AND TELEGRAPH CO.: This four and a quarter billion combine was organised by Morgan and is still under Morgan "management" control (the 20 largest stockholders own less than 5 per cent. of its total stock). 14 of its 19 directors, including the president and vice-president, are more or less closely linked by cross-directorships to Morgan concerns, and a Morgan partner is a director of two important subsidiaries. Management links are reinforced by banking relations. A Rockefeller minority interest is represented on the board by W. W. Aldrich.

2. WESTERN ELECTRIC CO.: Manufacturing subsidiary of A.T. & T.C. Markets sound film equipment through its subsidiary Electrical Research Products Inc. (ERPI). Western Electric equipment was until recently used under licence by all the major film companies except RKO.

3. GENERAL ELECTRIC CO.: Largest electrical manufacturers in the world. Organised by Morgan in 1892. Morgan still predominant, one Morgan partner and three other Morgan men on board.

4. CHASE NATIONAL BANK: Largest commercial bank in U.S.A. Controlled by John D. Rockefeller group since 1930. W. W. Aldrich, brother-in-law of J. D. Rockefeller, Jr., is president, two other members of the inner Rockefeller "cabinet" are board members. Rockefeller family has also substantial stock holding.

5. RADIO CORPORATION OF AMERICA: Incorporated in 1919 by G.E.C. to take over control of Marconi Co., and patent rights of G.E.C., Westinghouse Electric & Manufacturing Co., A.T. & T.C. and other concerns, Radio patent monopoly enforced under licensing system until 1930, when government anti-trust action led to a certain relaxation of control. The same action induced G.E.C. and Westinghouse to distribute their dominant stock interests to their stockholders, which implied a certain relaxation, though not elimination of control. At the same time Rockefeller interest became prominent and is still represented on the board (B. Cutler of Chase National Bank). Sound film equipment is produced and marketed through R.C.A. Photophone Co., which recently added Warner, 20th Century-Fox and Columbia to R.K.O. as its licencees.

covered, however, that the price demanded by his banking and telephone friends for this normal service was the abandonment on his part of control over his companies. Efforts to find alternative financial backing, although for a time apparently successful, proved fruitless in the end. Fox found himself face to face with a banking ring determined to wrest control from his hands and powerful enough to buy off even those bankers who at first were prepared to support him. After a long legal battle in which the telephone group attempted to throw the Fox concerns into receivership and which was further complicated by the filing of an anti-trust action against Fox on account of the Fox-Loew merger, the matter was finally settled by a victory of the telephone-banking ring. W. Fox sold out his voting stock for $18,000,000 to a business friend of the Halsey, Stuart firm, H. L. Clarke, a Chicago utilities magnate associated with the Insulls. Fox, who remained on the board of his former concerns for a short period after these events, offered the free use of his Tri-Ergon sound patents to these companies, but their new controllers preferred to enter into a licensing arrangement with the Western Electric interests at a cost to their shareholders of approximately $1,000,000 a year. (See Upton Sinclair Presents William Fox, p. 324.)

This part of the struggle between Fox and the telephone interests serves to illustrate the intimate inter-relation in the present financial position of the American film industry of the indirect form of patent control we have so far examined and the direct form of voting stock and management control to which we must now turn. It is necessary, however, at this point to stress the fact that here, as in any other sphere, control is not necessarily identical with ownership. The Fox case again provides a pertinent example. Prior to the change we have described control of these companies was vested exclusively in 5 per cent. of the total capital which alone carried voting rights (although W. Fox also owned a substantial block of non-voting shares). After the change the situation was even more striking: the Fox companies, then affiliated to Clarke's General Theatres Equipment Inc., were controlled by three voting trustees, each of whom owned only one share of stocks, the value of which in 1931 was a little over one third of a dollar. (See Sinclair *op. cit.*)

COMMENTS ON THE EIGHT MAJOR COMPANIES

The direct financial control of the eight major companies insofar as it could be ascertained from the information at present available in this country, is illustrated in Chart 2. Taking the companies one by one the following situation emerges :

PARAMOUNT : All the Paramount interests were merged in 1930 in a new company known as the Paramount Publix Corp., which continued the expansion operations of the group on a large

CHART 2.

DIRECT FINANCIAL CONTROL OR BACKING, 1936

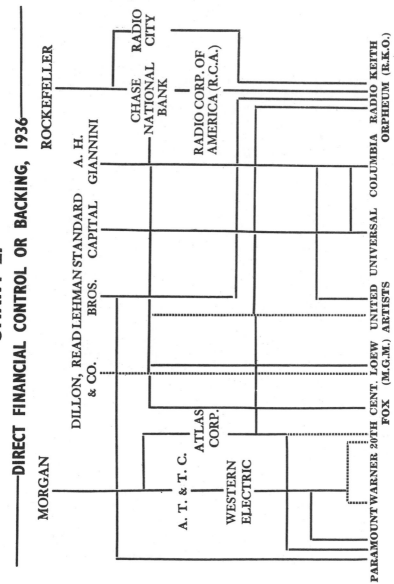

scale. Among other moves it acquired a controlling interest in the Columbia Broadcasting system, the second national radio service in the country, and established a production unit for talkies in France. In 1933 this company was thrown first into receivership and later into bankruptcy. It was reorganised in June, 1935, as Paramount Pictures Inc., control passing from Kuhn, Loeb & Co. to a group consisting of the Wall Street investment bankers Lehman Bros. and the Atlas Corporation, an investment trust within the Morgan sphere of influence. It appears that the Morgan telephone trust also acquired an interest in the company, and their influence was further strengthened by the appointment of J. E. Otterson, former chief of Erpi and prime mover in the struggle with Fox, to the controlling position of president of the new company.,

Commenting on this change Representative A. J. Sabath, chairman of the Congressional Committee investigating real estate bond reorganisation, stated : " The reorganisation of the Paramount Publix Corporation, now Paramount Pictures Inc., was marked by ' collusion, fraud and conspiracy '. This is a case where control of the company was grabbed by the American Telephone and Telegraph Company and other interests " (*New York Times*, 11th October, 1935). From the report into the company's affairs presented by J. P. Kennedy in June, 1936, and not made public until recently, it appears, however, that the new management did not materially improve the standards of efficiency of its predecessors. In the first place, after a preliminary survey, Mr. Kennedy considered it a waste of time and money to continue his enquiry, unless far-reaching changes in the management of the company were effected. " At the time when any well-managed picture business should be making substantial profits, Paramount is not making money and, as now managed, gives no hope of doing so," he wrote (see *Time*, 27th July, 1936). " While current unsatisfactory results are cumulative effects of a chain of incompetent, unbusinesslike and wasteful practices to be detected in every phase of production, this pervading incompetence is directly traceable to a lack of confidence in the management and direction of the company's affairs in the New York office."

One of the results of this report appears to have been the removal from the board of J. E. Otterson and his replacement by an experienced showman, B. Balaban. It would be a mistake, however, to conclude from such organisational changes that the ultimate Morgan control of the company had thereby been removed.

WARNER BROS.: The present financial control of this concern cannot be completely ascertained from the information at our disposal. The former banking affiliations, Goldman, Sachs & Co. and Hayden Stone & Co. appear to have been dropped, and it is reported that at one time Western Electric had an interest, though certainly not a controlling one, in the firm which is also tied up to some extent with R. Hearst. The situation in 1932 was that none of the Warner board members represented the giant interests (Morgan, Rockefeller, Mellon) with which we are mainly concerned in this section, but that the Guaranty Trust Co., Manufacturers' Trust Co., and New York Trust Co. (New York banks within the Morgan sphere of influence) were tied up with Warners as transfer agents and registrars for stock and as trustees and interest agents for bond issues.

TWENTIETH CENTURY-FOX: Shortly after the events we have described the General Theatres Equipment Inc. went into receivership which also affected the Fox Theatres Corp. Fox Films (the producing section of the Fox enterprises also controlling some of their theatre holdings) escaped receivership and was merged in 1935 with J. Schenck's Twentieth Century Corp. Chase National Bank which had backed Clarke retained the largest block of stock and probably the control of the concern after bearing a considerable proportion of the losses caused by the debacle of the old companies. This bank is now a Rockefeller concern, its president being W. W. Aldrich, brother-in-law of John D. Rockefeller, Jr., and the Rockefeller family also have a substantial stock interest in it. The Morgan interests are represented in Twentieth-Century-Fox by a minority holding of Atlas Corp.

LOEW'S INC.: In spite of the anti-trust action brought against Fox and later against General Theatres and of the nominal separation of Loew from Fox, the former company, ∕hose chief executive is N. M. Schenck, brother of J. Schenck, is also in the Chase National Bank—Rockefeller sphere of interest (through the stock purchased originally by W. Fox).

UNITED ARTISTS : Our information for this group is again incomplete. It should be remembered, however, that the producers collaborating in this organisation finance their own films, though the company owns a studio, runs a world-wide distributing organisation and controls a string of first run theatres. In the summer of 1936 the San Francisco banker, A. Giannini was elected chairman and president of the U.A. organisation. Twentieth-Century-Fox, and therefore indirectly the Rockefeller interests, have a 50 per cent. stock holding in United Artists Studios Inc. J. Schenck has also retained his presidency of United Artists Theatres of California Inc.

UNIVERSAL : In April, 1936, Universal Corp., a new holding company, acquired control of the Universal organisation through the purchase of common stock from Carl Laemmle and associates in accordance with an option originally given to Standard Capital

Co. and C. E. Rogers.   Over 90 per cent. of the common stock was
acquired for $5,500,000.   All the stock is held in a 10 year voting
trust of which the California banker, A. H. Giannini, the president
of Standard Capital, J. C. Cowdin, and the English miller, J. A.
Rank are prominent members.   J. C. Cowdin appears formerly to
have been vice-president of Blair & Co. and Bancamerica Blair Corporation (a prominent firm of investment bankers at one time allied
to Chase National Bank and also to Giannini), he is at present also
Chairman of Transcontinental Air Transport Inc., and director of
California Packing Corp., Curtiss-Wright Corp., Cheever Corp.,
Douglas Aircraft Corp., Whitehall Securities Co., Ltd., Sperry Gyro-
scope Co., Curtiss Aeroplane and Motor Co., Ford Instrument Co.,
Intercontinental Aviation Inc., Sperry Corp., and Waterbury Tool
Co. According to the English trade press the new Universal holding
company was formed through an agreement between Standard
Capital and an English syndicate headed by Lord Portal and
including also J. A. Rank.   This latter syndicate is concerned in
this country with the General Film Distributors Co., recently
organised by C. M. Woolf.   The Universal reorganisation provided
for a merger of their British subsidiary with G.F.D., and the
fact that J. A. Rank has been nominated a voting trustee, while
he and another British member are directors of the new American
holding company seems to indicate that the British interests have
acquired a share in the control of the American parent organisation.
In addition C. M. Woolf and H. Wilcox have been elected to the
board of the American production company.

RADIO-KEITH-ORPHEUM CORP.:   R.-K.-O., organised as we
have seen, in 1928 as a subsidiary of the Radio Corporation of
America, is the third of the great film companies falling into receivership during the recent crisis.   In October, 1935, R.C.A. sold half
its interest in R.-K.-O. to Atlas Corp. and Lehman Bros., who
also took an option for the purchase of the remainder.   It appears,
however, that the Rockefeller interest remains predominant in
R.-K.-O., through direct stock holdings in the name of Radio City,
the great Rockefeller real estate enterprise.

COLUMBIA: This company is at present controlled by a voting
trust holding 96 per cent. of the voting stock and consisting of
A. H. Giannini and two of the company's founders, Harry and
Jack Cohn.

CONCLUSION.

The development of American film finance which we have
attempted to outline in this brief sketch can be summarised as a
spiral movement from early monopoly control at a time when the
industry, measured by national standards, was but a minor sphere
of economic life and when its undreamed-of possibilities of expansion

threatened to be stifled by that monopoly hold, through a phase of meteoric expansion coupled with violent competition back again to monopoly control. It is a movement which is never for one moment basically deflected by the unceasing obligato of government anti-trust actions that enlivens its progress. Recently, as in the early years, the cry was raised that the bankers and big business men who were tending to oust the experienced showmen from the control of policy were ruining the industry, and there were hopes that a new move towards independent production might break the fetters of monopoly. But to-day the movie world is one of the major industries of the country and the control of its leading units has been concentrated both directly and indirectly in the hands of the most powerful financial groups in the United States, if not the capitalist world. To-day the movies are too valuable a prize for the men now in control to relinquish. And the recent changes in executive personnel to which we have referred indicates that the present rulers have learnt at least part of their lesson. But to-day, as from the first, the imponderabilia of box office appeal are the determining element for the industry's prosperity. Whether the movies will regain their former financial success ultimately depends on whether the Morgans and Rockefellers will find it to their interest in the unceasing change of American life to provide the masses with the type of pictures that alone will induce them to flock to their cinemas.

October, 1936.

SOURCES OF INFORMATION.

REPORT ON THE MOTION PICTURE INDUSTRY, National Recovery Administration, Works Materials No. 34, prepared by D. Bertrand, 1936.

B. B. HAMPTON, HISTORY OF THE MOVIES, 1931.

INTERNATIONAL MOTION PICTURE ALMANACK, 1936/7.

U. SINCLAIR, UPTON SINCLAIR PRESENTS WILLIAM FOX, n.d.

MOODY'S ECONOMIST SERVICES.

STANDARD STATISTICAL RECORDS.

A. ROCHESTER, RULERS OF AMERICA, 1936.

ASPECTS OF FILM

An Arno Press Collection

Adler, Mortimer J. **Art and Prudence.** 1937
Conant, Michael. **Anti-Trust in the Motion Picture Industry.** 1960
Croy, Homer. **How Motion Pictures Are Made.** 1918
Drinkwater, John. **The Life and Adventures of Carl Laemmle.** 1931
Hacker, Leonard. **Cinematic Design.** 1931
Hepworth, T[homas] C[raddock]. **The Book of the Lantern.** 1899
Johnston, Alva. **The Great Goldwyn.** 1937
Klingender, F.D. and Stuart Legg. **Money Behind the Screen.** 1937
Limbacher, James L. **Four Aspects of the Film.** 1969
Manvell, Roger, ed. **The Cinema 1950.** 1950
Manvell, Roger, ed. **The Cinema 1951.** 1951
Manvell, Roger, ed. **The Cinema 1952.** 1952
Marchant, James, ed. **The Cinema in Education.** 1925
Mayer, J.P. **British Cinemas and Their Audiences.** 1948
Sabaneev, Leonid. **Music for the Films.** 1935
Seabury, William Marston. **Motion Picture Problems.** 1929
Seldes, Gilbert. **The Movies Come from America.** 1937
U.S. House of Representatives, Committee on Education. **Motion Picture Commission: Hearings.** 1914
U.S. House of Representatives, Committee on Education. **Federal Motion Picture Commission: Hearings.** 1916
U.S. Senate, Temporary National Economic Committee. **Investigation of Concentration of Economic Power.** 1941
Weinberg, Herman G. **Josef von Sternberg.** 1967